HOT DAMN AND HELL YEAH

RECIPES FOR HUNGRY BANDITOS

TENTH ANNIVERSARY EXPANDED EDITION

Hot Damn and Hell Yeah
Recipes for Hungry Banditos
10th Anniversary Expanded Edition

Ryan Splint

First printing, March 17, 2015
All illustrations, recipes, and text are © Ryan Splint, 2015
This edition is © by Microcosm Publishing, 2015

Microcosm Publishing
2752 N Williams Ave
Portland, OR 97227

In the Vegan Cookbook series

For a catalog, write or visit
MicrocosmPublishing.com

ISBN 978-1-62106-989-8
This is Microcosm #186

Cover and design by Ryan Splint

Distributed in the United States and Canada by Legato / Perseus Books Group and in Europe by Turnaround.

This book was printed on post-consumer paper by union workers in the United States.

Dedicated:
To my folks, for teaching me how to cook at a young age and trusting me not to burn down the house while learning.

&

To all the friends who'd been to my place for a home-cooked meal ten years ago and told me I should write a cookbook.

FOREWORD

Howdy y'all,

A fair chunk of years ago, I moved from America to Australia, and in record time I found myself yearnin' fer the Tex-Mex and Southern food I grew up with. Livin' so far afield and maintainin' a vegan diet ta boot, meant figurin' it out on my own. My newfound Aussie crew, they got it inta my head that I should write a cookbook, so I did one—my way. Ten years later, I'm back in North America and reckon it's time ta saddle up for a final ride inta the sunset with *Hot Damn and Hell Yeah*. If you rode this trail with me before, you know what this chunk a' paper is all about. If not, here ya go:

Havin' a fair amount of experience in the kitchen under my belt didn't amount ta much when I set out to avoid havin' critters in my meals. As any folk who've tried will tell ya, there's a whole lotta bad vegetable-only food out there. Worse, there's a lot a' people that think pompous, self-righteous attitudes and morality lectures oughta be served alongside it, maybe ta make up for the lack of flavor in their food. It ain't too hard to see why vegan food and the people who eat it haven't wound up with the best of reputations.

But don't let that fool ya or put a scare into ya about what's comin' up.

This ain't about who's got a right to eat what, or what should and shouldn't be on yer plate for proper eatin'. Hell, it ain't even about healthy eating— recipes like Bourbon Whiskey BBQ Sauce (p.18), Corndawgs (p. 88), and the Confectionery and Dessert chapters oughta convince ya of that much.

What it *is* about is food without obscure ingredients, that're easy ta make and don't taste like sawdust even though it ain't chock-full a' dairy and meat. I've had ta wade through my share of bland and downright horrible food in order to learn how ta get by cookin' without meat or dairy. Now I ain't no master chef, but I figure I've done a decent job of it and wound up with some good recipes. Be a damn shame if I never got a chance to pass what ah've learned on ta other folks, so I've collected some of the best recipes I've ended up with, and finally wrote down others I've been making from scratch as situations have called for 'em. Now they're all yers fer the takin' and should work well for ya (maybe better if read usin' yer best southern accent, but no guarantees on that).

Now saddle up and let's get goin'!

TABLE OF CONTENTS

CONFECTIONERY

DESSERTS

A FEW TIPS FOR YA

One a' the hardest things I found when learnin' to cook food without meat or dairy was understandin' what half the ingredients in a lot of vegetarian recipes were, let alone where ya might find 'em. Ah s'pose sometimes people deadset on makin' food that's healthy plumb fergit that the rest of us gotta be able to decipher what they're puttin' in it. Last thing ya wanna do is travel to the ends a' the earth lookin' fer powdered root of something-or-other to complete yer dinner. Fer both yer sanity and mine, I stick to usin' simpler ingredients in my recipes, but some are still less commonly known or may be completely new to ya, so here they are:

TVP (TEXTURED VEGETABLE PROTEIN)
TVP is made from soy beans and usually sold as dehydrated granules—if mixed with hot water, it rehydrates and takes on the texture of minced beef. When used in yer cookin', I think you'll find it rare that people will notice it ain't the real thing. Ya shouldn't have too much trouble trackin' this down in the health food section of yer grocery store or nearly any whole foods store.

NUTRITIONAL YEAST
This is a yellow-brown, nearly powdered substance that usually shows up in recipes where yer after a cheesy flavor of some sort. Ya kin usually track this down at health food or whole food stores, but ah'll admit sometimes ya have a helluva time findin' it. Some folks might try sellin' you Brewer's Yeast instead, but don't fall fer that—it ain't even close to the same thing. Unfortunately, there's no decent substitute for Nutritional Yeast, so good luck huntin' it down.

SOY MILK
Soy milk is a made from pressed soy beans and is used in place of whole milk or buttermilk in recipes. Like normal milk, it curdles when mixed with a bit a' lemon juice so it's a great buttermilk substitute fer cookin' as well. Ya oughta have no trouble finding it in yer grocery store, as it's popular among the lactose-intolerant crowd. It's also usually fortified with extra vitamins so yer gettin' a bit of a nutritional bonus without havin' to lift a finger. I usually opt fer the vanilla-flavored type since it doesn't taste as chalky as the plain variety.

...ABOUT SUBSTITUTIONS

I feel ah've gotta at least warn ya about substitutin' ingredients in recipes. Like I said earlier, I aim ta make my food with basic ingredients and I have total confidence in 'em that way. I've seen some a' the simplest and tastiest recipes shot all ta hell 'cause someone tried substitutin' ingredients without understandin' what it'd do to the taste. Can't say I haven't made the same mistake myself, either. I encourage experimentin' with food— that's how most recipes here came about—but if yer itchin' to try doin' it with these recipes, keep that finger pointed squarely at yerself ta blame if ya wind up with a mouthful tastin' worse than dirt. I guarantee that ain't the case with these recipes, but if ya deviate from what's written then ya gotta take full responsibility for the results, fer better or worse.

CAROB VERSUS COCOA

Now I don't rightly know who started the idea of carob being a fine substitute fer cocoa, but those folks've got a lot ta answer for. I know I ain't the only one who's been suckered in by the promise of a tasty alternative to chocolate, only to be sorely disappointed and lookin' fer a rubbish bin. Carob ain't even in the same league as cocoa; hell, it comes from a completely different plant. Danged if I know what possessed folk to bill it as a good substitute. Ya won't find carob being used in any of the recipes here, and I discourage usin' it thinkin' you'll get a flavor tasting anywhere near as good. Carob is used in dog treats, and I don't know about y'all, but I've seen dogs eat some downright disturbin' things...keep that in mind next time yer considerin' the merits of carob versus cocoa in yer cookin'.

CANNED, FROZEN, OR FRESH VEGETABLES

Some of the recipes here, especially the soups and chilis, call fer vegetables ya kin buy fresh, frozen, or canned. Ya kin use any of them in yer recipes and the canned and frozen variety'll save ya time and worryin' about spoiled vegetables (one normal can of vegetables is equal to about 1 ½ C.). Just keep in mind how it'll affect yer cooking times and taste. Fresh vegetables will need to be cooked ta get 'em out of a raw state, but they'll have the best flavor and texture out've the three. Frozen vegetables will need to thaw and reheat while cooking, but they're almost as good as fresh vegetables for taste and texture. Canned vegetables are already cooked, but are usually packed in salt water and sometimes can take on the taste of the can because of it. What ya make up for in time with canned vegetables, ya tend ta lose in the taste and texture. In the end, no matter what ya use you'll still get a hearty meal and a full stomach so don't dwell on it much.

TOFU

Tofu is made from pressed soybeans and used as an alternative ta meat and dairy. It's sold packed in water, so you'll need to squeeze and drain it ta get the best results (see below). There are two main types you'll find poppin' up in here:

- FIRM TOFU -

Yep, this is a firm block of tofu, usually used instead a' beef or chicken in food. It's got a texture like a spongy cheese, and like a sponge you'll need to squeeze it out so it'll absorb flavor better when cookin' or marinatin'. Just take yer block of tofu out've the package and shake it over the sink, ta start with. Then, cut it into slices and lay them in a single layer on a clean dishtowel. Wrap the dishtowel (or two) around yer sliced tofu, lay it on the kitchen bench, place a heavy object on top (preferably a flat one, ta press it evenly) and leave it that way fer an hour or two. When ya return, the dishtowels should have soaked up most of the water and the tofu should feel a whole lot drier. Now it'll soak up flavor better when you cook or marinate it as a substitute fer beef or chicken in yer cookin'.

- SILKEN TOFU -

Silken tofu is also made from pressed soybeans, but the texture is completely different than firm tofu. It's useful in dips or as an egg substitute in pies or bread, but it also contains a lot more water that ya need to get rid of before using it. Otherwise, it'll turn whatever yer makin' into a soupy mess. Unfortunately, ya can't just squeeze it like ya do firm tofu—it'll just crumble inta watery slop if ya try. The best way I've come to get water outta silken tofu is cheesecloth. It may take a bit of time, but believe me pardner: it's better than spending the time to make food only ta have it ruined by too much moisture.

Get some cheesecloth from yer local grocery and place the silken tofu in the center of a square made from a few layers a' that. Pull the corners together and hold it by them as ya pick it up so the tofu is suspended in the center of the cheesecloth. Hold it over the sink and slowly twist the tofu in one direction, making the cheesecloth tighten around it. Water will start seepin' through the cheesecloth—wipe it off so it drips inta the sink and keep slowly twisting, wiping off the water as it comes out. Be patient and careful not to squeeze too hard, or you'll start squeezin' out tofu, too. Check how watery the tofu is, and continue gently squeezing the water out until it's considerably drier than what ya started with. It oughta resemble cottage cheese more than white jelly when yer done.

MEAT AND DAIRY

Luckily, food without meat and dairy ain't all salads, bread, and water like most folks think. Figurin' out what to substitute for meat and dairy in food was the hardest part of adjusting to cookin' this way. Here's how I sorted it all out for the recipes you'll find in here, in case ya wanna try convertin' recipes of yer own or switch some a' these to a meat and dairy variety:

THIS:	IS SUBSTITUTED WITH:
Beef	Firm Tofu marinated beef-style <u>or</u> TVP granules.
Chicken	Firm Tofu marinated chicken-style
Milk	Soy Milk
Buttermilk (1 C.)	1 C. Soy Milk mixed with 1 T. lemon juice
Egg (1)	Egg replacer powder (per directions) <u>or</u> 1/4 C. silken tofu, squeezed, and drained <u>or</u> 1 tsp. baking powder + 1/2 tsp. bi-carb soda + 2 T. flour + 3 T. water, mixed well

THERE ARE TWO KINDS OF PEOPLE IN THE WORLD, MY FRIEND: THOSE WITH A NAPKIN AROUND THEIR NECK, AND THE PEOPLE WHO HAVE THE JOB OF DOING THE COOKING.

SAUCES AND MIXES

WORCHESTERSHIRE SAUCE

Easy Worchestershire sauce ta make on yer own, without them pesky anchovies in it.

prep: 8 min | cook: 9 min | makes: 1 2/3 C.

1 C. apple cider vinegar
1/3 C. dark molasses
1/4 C. soy sauce
1/4 C. water
3 T. lemon juice
1 1/2 tsp. salt
1 1/2 tsp. mustard powder
1 tsp. onion powder
3/4 tsp. ground ginger
1/2 tsp. black pepper
1/4 tsp. dried garlic granules
1/4 tsp. cayenne pepper

Mix all ingredients in a saucepan and bring to a boil for 1-2 minutes to ensure powders and liquids blend. Allow the sauce to cool and transfer to a glass bottle for storage in yer fridge. Shake well before usin'.

CHEESE SAUCE

A mighty fine cheese-style sauce ta use on pasta, vegetables, Enchiladas (p. 77), Nachos (p. 76), or whatever else ya think of. Great for dippin' snacks in as well!

prep: 5 min | cook: 7 min | makes: 2 1/2 C.

1/3 C. nutritional yeast
1/2 C. all-purpose flour
1 T. dried onion
1/8 tsp. turmeric
1/8 tsp. white pepper (preferred) or black
6 T. olive oil
2 tsp. prepared American mustard
2 tsp. salt
1/2 C. tomato sauce or ketchup
1 3/4 water

Blend all ingredients well in a saucepan over medium-high heat, whisking continuously until it comes to a boil and thickens to your liking.

It'll thicken more as it cools, so it's best served hot or at least very warm. To reheat, add a bit of water and stir over low heat.

BEEF-STYLE MARINADE

In case yer lookin' to flavor firm tofu beef-style for somethin' like Fajitas (p. 76).

prep: 3 min   makes: 2 C.

3/4 C. soy sauce
1 C. water
1/4 C. white vinegar
1 1/2 tsp. garlic powder
1 1/2 tsp. ground ginger
1 tsp. black pepper (fresh-cracked if available)
1 tsp. beef or vegetable broth powder (optional)

Mix ingredients well; should do fer marinatin' a 350g package of firm/extra-firm tofu.

CHICKEN-STYLE MARINADE

Fer doin' a chicken-style firm tofu, like when makin' Country-Fried Tofu (p. 81)

prep: 4 min   makes: 2/3 C.

1/2 C. boiling water
1 tsp. white vinegar
2 T. soy sauce
2 1/2 T. vegetable broth powder (optional)
black pepper (to taste)
1/8 tsp. each of:
 - paprika
 - rosemary
 - garlic powder
 - onion powder
 - oregano
 - parsley
 - basil

Mix ingredients well and get ta marinatin' yerself 350g of firm or extra firm tofu.

Add extra water, vinegar, and soy sauce ta get yer tofu fully immersed if need be.

MUSHROOM GRAVY

A great all-purpose gravy ya kin use for mashed potatoes, Vegetable Pot Pie (p. 91), or wherever else a meal cries out in the night fer some hearty gravy.

prep: 5 min   cook: 15 min   makes: 2 C.

2 T. canola oil
1/2 C. onion, finely chopped
1/2 C. mushrooms, diced
3 T. nutritional yeast
1/4 tsp. salt
1 tsp. vegetable stock powder
black pepper, to taste (optional)
1/3 C. all-purpose flour
2 C. water

Heat oil in a saucepan over medium-high heat and sauté onions and mushrooms until onions are translucent.

Mix together spices and flour separately and then add to saucepan, stirring until oil and juices are absorbed and the onions and mushrooms are well-coated in the mix.

Add water 1/2 cup at a time, stirring well and allowing to thicken after each addition until all the water is added. Try fresh-cracked black peper to give it a bit of a kick.

EASY GRAVY

A simple, fast-food style gravy. Try it on Country-Style Biscuits (p. 26), a Vegetable Mountain (p. 92), or anything else ya might want ta slather in gravy.

prep: 10 min | cook: 15 min | makes: 3 C.

2 T. canola oil
4 T. all-purpose flour
3 C. broth of desired gravy flavor
1/4-1/2 tsp. salt (to taste)
1/4 tsp. black pepper
1/4 tsp. white sugar

Heat oil in a saucepan over medium heat and sprinkle in the flour, whisking well to remove any clumps.

Continue heating mixture until it turns a darker brown (7-10 minutes), stirring often to avoid scorching.

Add remaining ingredients, stir well, and increase heat until it comes to a boil.

Reduce heat and simmer until liquid reduces and gravy thickens to how ya like it.

CHILI GRAVY

This is called for if ya make Enchiladas (p. 77), but tasty on tex-mex any ol' time.

prep: 2 min   cook: 12 min   makes: 1 3/4 C.

1 T. canola oil
1/2 C. onion, chopped
1-3 tsp. chili powder (to taste)
1/8 tsp. salt
1 T. flour
1/4 tsp. garlic powder
1/2 tsp. cumin
3 T. tomato paste
1/8 tsp. cayenne pepper
1 C. chicken-flavored broth

Heat oil in a saucepan over medium-high heat and cook onion 'til it's translucent.

Mix spices and flour together and then stir in well with the onion, making sure there's no lumps and as much of the oil and moisture is absorbed as possible.

Mix tomato paste and broth together and pour inta the saucepan. Mix well and boil for a few minutes, stirring frequently to prevent any clumping or scorching.

Stir in extra flour to thicken more, or add extra spices to suit your taste if desired.

SALSA

Once ya make a batch a' this, you might not bother ever buyin' it pre-made again.

prep: 17 min   cook: 40 min   makes: 4 C.

1 1/2 C. diced tomatoes
1 1/2 C. water
1/2 C. green bell pepper, chopped
1/2 C. red bell pepper, chopped
1 small red onion, chopped
1 stalk celery, finely chopped
1/3 C. tomato paste
1/4 tsp. salt
2 T. white vinegar
1/4 tsp. dried garlic granules
1/4 C. jalapeno peppers, chopped—this'll make yer salsa MEDIUM HOT

   - use 2 T. jalapenos for MILD - use 1/3 C. jalapenos for HOT

Combine all ingredients in a saucepan over medium-high heat. Bring to a boil, then reduce heat and simmer for 30 minutes or until thickened. Cool, then transfer to a storage container and refrigerate overnight to let the flavors combine before usin'.

15

BLACK BEAN SALSA

A different style a' salsa, more fer snackin' on with tortilla chips rather than usin' fer main meals. Once ya taste it, though, ya might wanta try it on a burrito or two.

prep: 20 min   makes: 4 C.

1 1/2 C. black beans, cooked and drained
1/2 C. corn kernels, cooked and drained
1/2 red onion, chopped
1 C. tomatoes, seeded and chopped
1/2 C. green onions, chopped
1/2 C. cilantro, chopped
1/2 red bell pepper, chopped (optional)
1 1/2 tsp. white vinegar
1 T. + 1 1/2 tsp. lime juice
1/4 tsp. black pepper
1/2 tsp. cumin
1/4 tsp. salt

Combine all ingredients in a large bowl and toss well. Transfer to a storage container and refrigerate overnight to allow flavors to blend. Toss well again before serving.

CHILI RELLENO DIP

A tangy dip ideal fer tortilla chips ta work inta yer snacking habits

prep: 10 min   makes: 4 C.

2 tomatoes, chopped
3 green onions, chopped
1/2 C. black olives, chopped
1/2 C. green chili peppers (canned), chopped
3 T. olive oil
1 1/2 T. red wine vinegar
1 tsp. garlic powder
1/2 tsp salt
1/2 tsp. pepper

Mix all ingredients together and chill before servin' with corn chips.

GUACAMOLE

Ah, good ol' Guacamole . . . this'll pop up as a toppin fer Enchiladas (p. 77), and Nachos (p. 76), but whip it up fer any burritos, tacos, corn chips, or what have ya.

prep: 10 min   makes: 2 C.

2 ripe avacados
1 clove garlic, crushed
1 tsp. lemon juice
1/2 tsp. salt
1/4 tsp. black pepper
1/8 tsp. cayenne pepper
1 T. olive oil (optional)
1/2 C. green onions, chopped (optional)
1 tomato, seeded and chopped (optional)

Cut avocados in half and remove pits.

Spoon out avocado from skins and mash with a fork in a medium-sized bowl (it don't haveta be a smooth paste—lumps give it that homemade charm).

Add crushed garlic, lemon juice, spices, and oil, mixing well after each addition.

Fold in any other ingredients and refrigerate covered until yer ready ta use it.

ALMOST SOUR CREAM

This won't fool ya next ta the real thing, but it works well alongside other toppings like Guacamole (p. 17), and Salsa (p. 15) for Nachos (p. 76), or Enchiladas (p. 77).

prep: 12 min   makes: 1 C.

Food processor or blender
1 300g package firm silken tofu (1 1/2 C.)
1 T. canola oil
2 tsp. lemon juice
2 tsp. apple cider vinegar
1 tsp. white sugar
1/2 tsp. salt

Squeeze and drain silken tofu well.

Combine all ingredients except oil in yer food processor or blender and let 'er rip.

Add oil a bit at a time, blending all the while fer several minutes until it thickens up.

Refrigerate in an airtight container fer up to a week and use while fresh—this gem can't survive in a freezer, unfortunately.

SAUCES AND MIXES
SOY MAYONNAISE

This'll easily match or beat the taste of soy mayo ya might find at yer general store.

prep: 15 min   makes: 1 C.

Food processor or blender
1 300g package firm/extra firm silken tofu
2 tsp. cider vinegar
2 tsp. lemon juice
1 tsp. white sugar
1/2 tsp. dijon mustard
1/2 tsp. salt
1 1/2-2 T. canola oil

Squeeze and drain silken tofu well.

Place all ingredients except oil inta yer blender or food processer and puree the contents on high speed a few minutes, until smooth.

Add oil—halfa Tablespoon at a time—blending a few minutes after each addition until ya got a thicker, creamier texture.

Store in the refrigerator fer up to a week—not suitable fer freezin'.

BOURBON WHISKEY BBQ SAUCE

Ya might be lookin' ta just drink this, but it's actually a mighty fine BBQ sauce too.

prep: 7 min   cook: 30 min   makes: 1 C.

1/4 C. Worcestershire Sauce (p. 12)
1/4 C. onion, minced
4 cloves garlic, minced
3/4 C. bourbon whiskey
2 C. ketchup or tomato sauce
1/4 C. tomato paste
1/3 C. apple cider vinegar
1/2 tsp. Tabasco sauce
1/2 C. brown sugar
1/2 tsp. black pepper
1 1/2 tsp. salt

Sauté onion and garlic with the bourbon in a saucepan over medium-high heat until onion is translucent.

Add remaining ingredients, mix well, and bring to a boil. Reduce heat and simmer 20 minutes, stirring occasionally to prevent scorching. Strain or puree if ya want a chunkier or smoother consistency (respectively). Refrigerate in an airtight container.

CORNMEAL BATTER

In case ya got a hankerin' for deep-frying Corn Dawgs (p. 88), or some such eats.

prep: 7 min   makes: 3 C.

1 C. cornmeal
1 C. all-purpose flour
1/4 C. white sugar
3 tsp. baking powder
1/4 tsp. salt
1/8 tsp. black pepper
1 C. soy milk
1 egg substitute :
 (mix well before adding)
   1 tsp. baking powder
   + 1/2 tsp. baking soda
   + 2 T. all-purpose flour
   + 3 T. water

Mix dry ingredients together well, then add soy milk and egg substitute. Stir only well enough to blend wet and dry ingredients, overmixin' will thicken up the batter more than is useful.

If too thick to work easily with, try adding one tablespoon of water or soy milk and mix well, add another tablespoon of liquid if needed.

SOUTHERN-FRIED SPICE MIX

A mix of spices to use fer Country-Fried Tofu (p. 81), or other spicy, fried endeavors.

prep: 7 min   makes: ~ 3 C.

2 C. all-purpose flour
1/2 tsp. each of:
   - salt
   - thyme
   - dried basil
   - dried oregano
1 T. each of:
   - celery salt
   - black pepper
   - mustard powder
4 T. paprika
2 T. sugar
2 tsp. garlic salt
1 tsp. ground ginger

Mix all ingredients together and store in a large, airtight container 'til needed.

CAJUN SPICE MIX

You'll need this spicy mix for Red Beans and Rice (p. 50) or yer own cajun recipes.

prep: 2 min   makes: 1/4 C.

2 1/2 tsp. paprika
2 tsp. garlic powder
1 tsp. salt
1 teaspoon cayenne pepper
1 teaspoon black pepper
1 teaspoon onion powder
1 1/4 tsp. dried oregano
1 1/4 tsp. dried thyme
1/2 tsp. red pepper flakes

Mix all the ingredients well and store in an airtight container ta keep dry fer use.

BREADS

I don't know about you, but I find coming in from the cold to a warm house filled with the scent of fresh-made breads one of the most comforting things in life. Even with the rising demand for gluten-free eatin' and low-carbohydrate diet fads out there, homemade breads will have a place on my homestead 'til the very end.

Tortillas (pps.22 and 23) are essential fer some recipes in this book, but before ya drive yerself mad tryin' ta roll 'em out easily, here's the best way ta go about it:

1. Take a gallon-size zip-style plastic bag and slice it up the sides, leavin' the bottom edge intact.

2. Lay the plastic flat on yer work surface and place a ball of yer tortilla dough in the center of one side and fold the other side of the plastic overtop the ball of dough .

3. Roll the dough out in all directions between the plastic (lift the plastic off and lay it flat again if it wrinkles up).

4. With yer tortilla now rolled out between the layers of plastic, remove the top layer of plastic, then peel the tortilla off the bottom layer and dust with a bit of flour and set it aside fer cookin'.

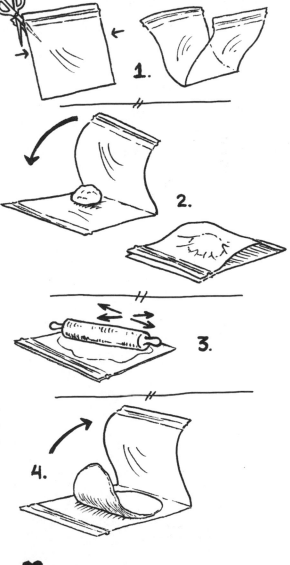

FLOUR TORTILLAS

These are downright essential fer Burritos (pgs. 73, 74), Fajitas (p. 76), Enchiladas (pgs. 77, 78), and even some desserts (p. 122), never mind the snackin' uses!

prep: 1 hr 25 min | cook: 25 min | makes: 6-8 tortillas

2 1/2 C. all-purpose flour
1 tsp. salt
1/4 C. margarine or oil
3/4 C. boiling water

Stir flour and salt together in a large bowl. Rub the margarine in by hand until evenly mixed, then hollow out a well in the center of your ingredients and pour the boiling water into it. Mix well with a wooden spoon until you've got a doughy texture that's cooled down enough to work with hands (shouldn't take long).

Sprinkle flour on top and knead the dough with your hands until it's a smooth consistency without sticking to yer fingers.

Roll pieces of dough into 2 inches/5 cm balls, place on a tray, and cover 'em with a towel. Leave covered an hour or more before movin' on.

Roll the dough balls out on a lightly floured surface to the thickness yer after, then get a skillet or griddle warmed up over high heat.

Place a tortilla on your cooking surface for about ten seconds. Flip over as soon as you see a bubble or two formin' on top.

Cook 20–30 seconds then flip back over to cook the other side 20–30 seconds; keep a close eye on 'em—you want them cooked soft with light brown spots, not crispy with dark brown spots.

Stack cooked tortillas on a plate covered with a dish towel to keep soft until you're ready for 'em. Leftovers can be refrigerated or frozen alright.

CORN TORTILLAS

Now ya may not find these as tasty or commonly used as the flour variety, but this recipe'll make six corn tortillas that you'll need ta make Enchiladas (p. 23) fer yer gang.

prep: 50 min | cook: 15 min | makes: 6 tortillas

3/4 C. cornmeal
3/4 C. all-purpose flour
1/4 tsp. salt
1 tsp. baking powder
1/2 C. boiling water

Stir dry ingredients together in a large bowl until well-mixed.

Stir in the boiling water to form a brittle dough, then knead with your hands until the dough holds together and you get a smoother consistency. It might still feel a bit rough, but that'll just from the grittier cornmeal, so don't worry none.

Divide and roll the dough into six balls, then place them on a tray and cover with a towel or plastic wrap fer about 30 minutes ta rest and allow the cornmeal to absorb moisture and soften up fer rolling out..

Flatten each ball into a disc shape, then roll out on a lightly floured surface, or between layers of a plastic freezer bag (the trick demonstrated on page 21) to get a larger, thinner tortilla.

Heat a lightly oiled skillet over medium heat and cook each tortilla until light brown on each side. You can do this by only cooking twenty seconds at a time on each side, constantly flipping 'em over until they're evenly cooked.

Keep cooked tortillas covered on a plate until you're ready to use 'em.

CORNBREAD

Cornbread is a must-have when eatin' Chilis (pgs. 65-67), or Cajun-style food (p. 50), but try it with a bit of honey or jam for a treat—it's that good all by itself.

prep: 20 min | cook: 20-25 min | makes: 16 servings

2 C. all-purpose flour
3/4 C. cornmeal
1 T. baking powder
dash of cayenne pepper (optional)
2/3 C. white sugar
1 tsp. salt
1/3 C. margarine, softened
1 tsp. vanilla extract
1 1/3 C. soy milk
2 egg substitutes:
 (mix together well before adding)
    2 tsp. baking powder + 1 tsp. baking soda
    + 1/4 C. all-purpose flour + 6 T. water

Preheat oven to 400° F (200° C) and coat an 8-inch (20 cm) baking pan lightly with cooking spray or margarine.

In a medium bowl, mix together flour, cornmeal, baking powder, and the dash of cayenne pepper if you've chosen ta use it.

In a separate large bowl, beat together the sugar, salt, margarine, and vanilla extract until creamy. Stir in yer egg substitutes one at a time, mixing well after each.

Alternate stirring the flour mixture and soy milk into the sugar mixture, beating well after each addition.

Pour batter into yer greased pan and bake in the preheated oven fer 20-25 minutes, until golden brown and a toothpick or knife stuck inta the center comes out clean.

HUSH PUPPIES

These li'l Cajun-style breads suit Red Beans and Rice (p. 50), or Chilis (pgs. 65-67) nicely, or hold their own as an appetizer before a hearty, spicy meal.

prep: 25 min | cook: 15 min | makes: 16 servings

1 C. cornmeal
1/2 C. all-purpose flour
1/2 tsp. salt
1/2 tsp. baking powder
1/4 tsp. baking soda
1/2 tsp. cayenne pepper
1/4 tsp. garlic powder
1/8 tsp. black pepper
1/8 tsp. chili powder (or to taste)
1/4 C. parsley, fincly chopped
1/2 C. green onions, finely chopped
1/2 C. soy milk mixed with 1 1/2 tsp. lemon juice
1 T. canola oil
2 egg substitutes :
 (mix together well before adding)
    2 tsp. baking powder + 1 tsp. baking soda
    + 1/4 C. all-purpose flour + 6 T. water

In a large bowl, combine all dry ingredients and blend well. Add the remaining ingredients, mixing well after each addition.

Form the mixture inta spoon-sized balls and deep fry in oil until golden brown, or if ya don't have a fryer, press inta patties and fry in a skillet well-coated with oil.

COUNTRY-STYLE BISCUITS

Quick and easy buttermilk-style biscuits, good for Biscuits and Gravy (p. 81),
split and topped with jam or yer favorite spread fer noon or night-time eatin'.

prep: 17 min | cook: 10-15 min | makes: six 3-inch biscuits

2 C. all-purpose flour
1 T. baking powder
1 tsp. salt
3 T. cold margarine
2/3 C. soy milk mixed with 2 tsp. lemon juice

There's a couple tricks ta gettin' the most outta these classic biscuits:
- Make sure the margarine is cold enough to cut in without softening too much before baking (try chilling it in the freezer if ya gotta). You'll get nicer texture and rise when it melts in the oven rather than the mixin' bowl or in yer hands.
- Go easy on 'em! Don't overmix or overwork yer dough when the liquid is mixed in, that'll just toughen up yer biscuits. Mix just enough to moisten the dry ingredients and be gentle when ya flatten out the dough for cuttin'.

Preheat oven to 400° F (200° C) and lightly grease a baking tray.

Combine flour, baking powder, and salt together in a medium-sized bowl.

Cut margarine into flour mixture with a couple knives or a pastry blender until you've got a crumbly mixture ta work with. Keep yer hands out've it for now (as per above).

Stir in the soy milk mixture until liquid is absorbed and a rough dough is formed. It should hold together enough ta handle, but not stick to yer fingers or the bowl.

Scrape dough out onto a lightly floured surface and knead a few times.

Pat or roll out to a 1/2-inch (1 1/4 cm) thickness, and cut into circles using a biscuit cutter, empty can, or any other improvised cutter of the size ya'd like.

Bake in preheated oven for 10-15 minutes until lightly browned. Serve pipin' hot!

PANCAKES

Serve these up any ol' time of day, but fergit them "syrup-flavored"
toppings—go the extra mile with 100% maple syrup ta have 'em taste best!

prep: 11 min | cook: 14 min | makes: 8 pancakes

1 C. all-purpose flour
1/2 tsp. salt
2 1/2 tsp. baking powder
2 T. white sugar
dash of nutmeg (optional)
2 T. margarine, melted
1 C. soy milk mixed with 1 T. lemon juice
2 egg substitutes—mix together well before adding:
    2 tsp. baking powder + 1 tsp. baking soda
    + 1/4 C. all-purpose flour + 6 T. water

Sift all the dry ingredients together in a medium-sized bowl. In a separate bowl, mix the wet ingredients together. Stir wet ingredients into the dry ingredients just until blended—overmixin' won't get you anything but tough pancakes, pardner.

Grease a skillet or griddle with non-stick cooking spray or margarine and place over medium-high heat.

Pour batter into skillet just shy of 1/3 C. at a time and cook until bubbles slow down and they're lightly browned on the bottom, then flip with a thin spatula and cook the other side. Add more grease to the cookin' surface between batches if need be.

Stack and serve warm — slip a bit a' margarine between each fer good measure!

CRANBERRY SCONES

These are good eatin' fer lazy mornings at the bandito hideout.
prep: 20 min | cook: 15 min | makes: 12 servings

2 C. all-purpose flour
1 T. baking powder
1/2 tsp. baking soda
2 T. white sugar
1/4 tsp. salt
1 tsp. grated lemon rind
1/2 C. margarine
1/2 C dried cranberries
2/3 C. soy milk mixed with 2 tsp. lemon juice

Like Country-Style Biscuits (p. 26), make sure the margarine is cold enough to cut in without softening too much before baking. This'll ensure ya get a nice texture and rise when these are bakin' in the oven.

Preheat oven to 425° F (220° C). Combine dry ingredients except cranberries in a large bowl.

Cut margarine into dry ingredients with two knives or a pastry blender, until mixture is crumbly. Add dried cranberries and toss lightly to coat 'em with the mix.

Add soy milk mixture and stir just until dry ingredients are moistened to form dough.

Turn out dough onto a lightly floured surface, and gently knead five, or six times.

Divide dough in half and shape each half into a ball. Gently flatten both balls into seven-inch (18 cm) circles on an ungreased baking sheet.

Use a knife to indent three deep lines through each circle to create six wedges, but don't cut clear through—these'll break right off nicely once they're properly baked.

Bake in preheated oven for 10-15 minutes, until lightly browned. Transfer as a whole to wire racks to cool slightly, *then* break 'em into wedges.

PUMPKIN BREAD

Taste this moist bread warm on a cold day and you're liable ta eat it all in one sittin'.

prep: 25 min | cook: 75 min | makes: 1 loaf

2 C. pumpkin, cooked and pureed (or canned)
1/4 C. canola oil
1/2 C. silken tofu
1 C. white sugar
2 C. all-purpose flour
2 tsp. baking powder
1 tsp. baking soda
1/2 tsp. ground cinnamon
1/2 tsp. ground nutmeg
1/4 tsp. ground cloves
1/4 tsp. ground ginger
1/2 C. raisins
1/2 C. walnuts, chopped

Preheat oven to 350° F (175° C). Grease a loaf pan, dusting lightly with extra flour.

Squeeze and drain silken tofu well, and puree or mash as smooth as possible.

In a large bowl, mix pumpkin, oil, tofu, and sugar together until smooth.

In a separate bowl, mix together the flour, baking powder, baking soda, and spices.

Stir the flour mixture into the pumpkin mixture until just blended. Stir in the raisins and walnuts until even distributed, then pour the batter into the prepared loaf pan.

Bake in the center of the oven for 60-75 minutes or a knife inserted into center of loaf comes out clean—allow to cool in pan for 10 minutes then cool on a wire rack.

ZUCCHINI BREAD

One a' the best things about summer is how much zucchini ya see on offer. Get yer hands on some and whip up some of this bread fer hot or cold snackin'.

prep: 25 min | cook: 60 min | makes: 1 loaf

1 1/2 C. all-purpose flour
1 1/2 tsp. baking powder
1 tsp. baking soda
1/2 tsp. cocoa
1/2 tsp. salt
1/2 tsp. cinnamon
1/8 tsp. allspice
1/2 C. canola oil
1/2 C. white sugar
2 T. brown sugar
1 T. lemon juice
1/4 C. silken tofu
1/4 C. water
1 C. zucchini, grated/
  shredded

Preheat oven to 350° F (175° C). Grease yer loaf pan and dust lightly with flour.

Squeeze and drain silken tofu well, and puree or mash as smooth as possible.

In a large bowl, mix together flour, baking powder, baking soda, cocao, and spices.

In a medium bowl, mix tofu, sugars, lemon juice, oil, and water together until sugars dissolve and mix is smooth—you can use the sugar to grind the silken tofu into a smooth paste against the sides of the bowl before adding the liquid ingredients.

Add yer wet ingredients into the bowl of dry ingredients and mix until combined and liquid is well distributed—there should be no dry ingredients in the mix any more.

Mix the grated zucchini into yer batter and scrape it into your prepared loaf pan. The batter will be plenty thick, but don't you worry none—it'll cook up just fine.

Bake in the center of the oven for 50-60 minutes or a knife inserted into center of loaf comes out relatively clean (moist is okay, coated with batter ain't).

Allow the bread to cool in the loaf pan for ten minutes then turn it out of the pan to finish cooling on a wire rack.

Serve warm or cold, it oughta taste great either way.

BANANA BREAD

A classic quick bread, makin' the most of natural sugars found in overripe 'naners.

prep: 25 min | cook: 50-60 min | makes: 1 loaf

3 very ripe bananas (and I mean brown and squishy, pardner!)
2 C. all-purpose flour
2 tsp. baking powder
1/2 tsp. salt
1/2 tsp. cinnamon
1/8 tsp. nutmeg
1/2 C. firm silken tofu
1/4 C. margarine
1/2 C. white sugar
1/4 C. brown sugar
1/2 tsp. vanilla extract
1/2 C. walnuts, chopped (optional)

Preheat oven to 350° F (175° C). Grease a loaf pan and lightly dust with flour.

Squeeze and drain the silken tofu and puree or mash as smooth as possible. Set aside.

Peel and mash the bananas and also set aside for a minute, ain't quite for 'em yet.

In a medium bowl, mix together flour, baking powder, salt, cinnamon, and nutmeg.

In a large bowl, mix the margarine and sugars together until creamy. Add tofu and use the sugars to grind the tofu against the side of the bowl to make smooth.

Add the mashed bananas and vanilla to the tofu mixture and and beat well to blend.

Stir the flour mix into the bowl of liquid ingredients a bit at a time, mixing until just combined and moisture is absorbed.

Fold in walnuts if ya decided on usin' 'em, then scrape it all outta the bowl and inta yer prepared loaf pan.

Bake 50-60 minutes, until the top is golden and a toothpick or knife inserted into the middle of the pan comes out reasonably clean—it's alright for it ta bring along some moist crumbs, but ya don't want it still covered in batter.

Remove from oven and leave in pan another 10 minutes before dumpin' out onta yer wire rack to finish coolin'.

CLASSIC DROP BISCUITS

When it comes ta bread, it don't get a whole lot easier than drop biscuits! Suitable fer eatin' with just about any chili or stew, gravy, or alone with jam and margarine.

prep: 10 min | cook: 10-15 min | makes: 6 servings

1 C. all-purpose flour
1 1/2 tsp. white sugar
1 1/4 tsp. baking powder
1/4 tsp. salt
1/2 C. soy milk
1/4 tsp. cold margarine

Like Cranberry Scones (p. 28) and the Country-Style Biscuits (p. 26) before them, cold margerine that's cut in without softening too much before baking is the secret to makin' the puppies as best they can be—don't dawdle!

Preheat oven to 450° F (230° C) and have a cookie sheet or baking tray standin' by.

Mix the flour, sugar, baking powder, and salt together in a medium bowl.

Cut the cold margarine into the flour mixture with a pastry blender or a couple a' knives until it resembles coarse crumbs or small pebbles.

Add soy milk and mix well until all dry ingredients are evenly moistened and any remaining moisture is absorbed—it oughta resemble wet dough or really thick batter.

Scoop out a heaped spoonful of batter and drop it on yer cookie sheet, spacing five more heaped spoonfuls around the cookie sheet.

Bake in preheated oven for 10-15 minutes, until the tops start turnin' golden brown.

Cool on a wire rack before cartin' 'em off to whatever tasty fate is in store for 'em.

HERB AND CHEESE DROP BISCUITS

Savory drop biscuits that go well with soups, chilies, or as a side to any hearty meal.

prep: 10 min | cook: 10 min | makes: 6 servings

1 1/2 C. all-purpose flour
3 T. nutritional yeast flakes
1 1/2 tsp. baking powder
1/2 tsp. salt
1/2 tsp. sage
1/2 tsp. parsley flakes
1/4 tsp. onion powder
1/4 tsp. garlic powder
dash of black pepper
3/4 C. + 2 T. soy milk
1/4 C. cold margarine

Preheat the oven to 450° F (230° C) and grease a cookie sheet or baking tray.

In medium-sized bowl, combine all dry ingredients and mix well.

Cut the cold margarine into the flour mixture with a pastry blender or two knives, until it looks like a bowl of coarse crumbs or margarine is the size of small pebbles.

Add the soy milk to the flour mixture and mix well, until the liquid is totally absorbed and there are no orphaned piles of dry ingredients sitting in yer bowl.

Drop the dough by heaped spoonfuls onto the greased cookie sheet, makin' six (6) evenly spaced clumps of dough ready to be baked fer all they're worth.

Bake in the oven for 10-12 minutes, until biscuits turn golden brown on top. Careful not to let the tips start to burn, that's a surfire sign ya gotta pull 'em outta there.

Remove from oven and cool on a wire rack.

Serve warm with soup or chili and watch 'em get devoured by any hungry varmints you've invited inta yer home.

CINNAMON AND RAISIN DROP BISCUITS

A quck and easy sweet biscuit option ta get ya movin' in the morning.
prep: 10 min | cook: 10-15 min | makes: 6 servings

1 1/2 C. all-purpose flour
1/4 C. white sugar
3/4 tsp. salt
1/2 tsp. cinnamon
1 1/2 tsp. baking powder
1/4 C. cold margarine
1/3 C. raisins
3/4 C. soy milk

Preheat oven to 425° F (220° C) and get yer reliable ol' cookie sheet out and ready.

In a medium bowl, mix flour, sugar, salt, cinnamon, and baking powder together well.

Cut in the cold margarine with a pastry blender or two knives until it resembles coarse crumbs or small pebbles. Add raisins and mix well to distribute evenly throughout.

Add soy milk and mix until it is completely absorbed and the mixture resembles a loose dough or very thick batter, one suitable for scoopin' out ta drop elsewhere!

Havin' said that, scoop out a heaped spoonful (about 1/6th of yer dough) and drop it onto yer cookie sheet. Scoop out the remaining five spoonfuls and drop evenly around the cookie sheet and then pop the whole thing inta yer preheated oven.

Bake 10-15 minutes, until golden brown but before the tips start ta' burn. Cool on a wire rack, then break open to smother with margarine or jam and dig in!

SWEET POTATO DROP BISCUITS

Yet another tasty use fer sweet potatoes ta fill yer belly any time a' day.

prep: 15 min | cook: 20-25 min | makes: 6 servings

1 1/4 C. all-purpose flour
2 1/2 tsp. baking powder
1 tsp. baking soda
1/4 tsp. salt
1/4 C. cold margarine
1/2 C. soy milk mixed with
1 1/2 tsp. lemon juice
1/2 C. sweet potato, cooked and mashed
2 T. white sugar
2 T. brown sugar

Preheat oven to 400° F (200° C) and grease a cookie sheet lightly with margarine.

In a large bowl, mix together the flour, baking powder, baking soda, and salt.

Cut the margarine into the flour mixture with a pastry blender or two knives until the mix resembles coarse crumbs or at least small pebbles a' margarine mixed all about.

In a medium bowl, whisk the soy milk mixture with the sugars until they dissolve, then add the mashed sweet potatoes and mix well until it's a smooth liquid ta use.

Add the liquid mixture into the dry ingredients and mix well until the dry ingredients are fully moistened and you've got a bit of a floppy, sludgy dough starin' back at ya.

Scoop dough out in six heaped spoonfuls, spaced evenly on yer greased cookie sheet.

Bake for 20-25 minutes in preheated oven, until turning golden brown on top.

Cool on a wire rack before devourin' fer breakfast, lunch, dinner, or just a snack.

YEAST BREADS

I seem to meet a lotta folks too intimidated by the thought of workin' with yeast to ever try it out. Rest assured, pardner—there's no need ta fear yeast breads!

Sure, ya might make a mess of things the first try or two, but when do ya ever get something perfect the first time 'round? Roll up them sleeves and get yerself some hands-on experience—I'm no professional, but I get by with the following techniques I use. Trust me, it'll open up a whole new world of possibilities for ya!

Kneading is the first word likely ta make folks skittish about yeast breads, but the only kneading I ask ya ta do is fer getting the remaining flour needed inta yer doughs. Ain't no ten minutes of kneading dough in yer future with me, amigo!

1. Put ycr ball or clump dough on a lightly floured work surface and pat it down slightly into an oval or circle, then fold the dough in half towards ya and press it down ta stick to itself.

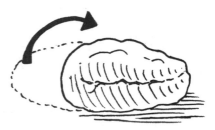

2. Use the heel of yer hand to push it down and away from ya—not straight down and not straight away, but like yer hand is attached to a wheel about ta roll back wards on the ground. Turn the dough a quarter turn, then fold it towards ya again, press it down and away again, turn it another quarter turn and repeat until the rest of the flour is incorporated inta the dough, dusting yer work surface (and yer hands) with flour as needed ta do that.

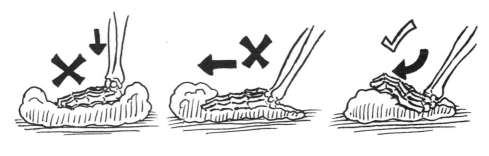

NOPE   NOPE   YEP.

Folding is about the easiest ta follow, being pretty much all it says it is.

1. Place yer ball of dough on a lightly floured work surface and press it down into a circle. Grab one side of the dough and stretch it to the side until it's long enough ta fold back across the dough and be stuck down about two-thirds of the way across yer chunk of dough. Now do the same fer the opposite side:

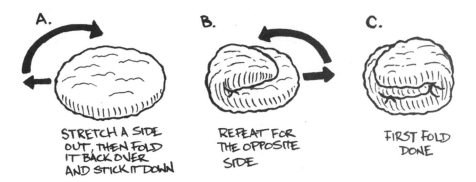

A. STRETCH A SIDE OUT, THEN FOLD IT BACK OVER AND STICK IT DOWN

B. REPEAT FOR THE OPPOSITE SIDE

C. FIRST FOLD DONE

2. Rotate yer dough one quarter turn (90 degrees) and do the same thing ya did in the first step - stretch each side out and back over the dough:

A. ¼ ROTATE DOUGH 1/4 TURN

B. STRETCH A SIDE OUT AND FOLD IT BACK OVER

C. REPEAT FOR THE OPPOSITE SIDE

3. With each side of yer dough folded over one another, you're done - flip the folded dough over so the last fold is held down by the weight of the dough and yer ready to leave it rising for the next step in yer bread-making.

NOW FLIP YER FOLDED DOUGH OVER...

...AND IT'S READY TO RISE

Shaping might take a bit of practice, but you'll be an old hand at it in no time.

1. Place the ball of dough down on a lightly floured surface and dust yer hands and the dough with a bit more flour if the dough sticks to yer hands too much. Cup yer hands over the dough and user yer fingerstips ta press and stretch the edges on opposite sides around the bottom of the dough and then clutch yer fingers underneath ta stick the stretched edges to the bottom of the dough.

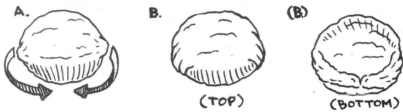

2. Turn the dough slightly ta cup yer hands on the dough next ta where ya just stretched the edges under, and repeat the process—push the dough around underneath with yer fingertips and stick the stretched dough to the bottom of the ball. Picture yerself shaping a mushroom cap.

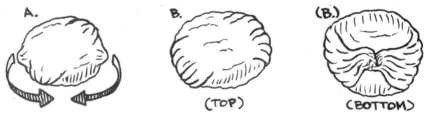

3. Once you've done this all the way around the edges of the dough, you'll notice the top of the dough is tighter and firmer then ya started with from streching it under. Now lift the dough up and scrunch any lumps of the stretched edges on the bottom together into the center of the bottom and pinch them all together tightly to seal, then flatten that clump up into the bottom of the dough.

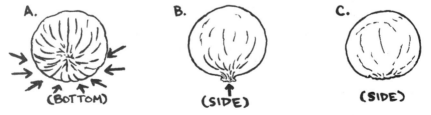

4. If you're baking in a loaf pan, dust your hands and dough again, then gently pull in opposite directions to stretch the ball into a pill shape to fit the pan.

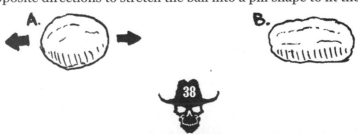

BIG OL' PRETZELS

Giant pretzels like ya find sold at the County Fair next ta Corn Dawgs (p. 88).

prep: 2 hr 30 min | cook: 10 min | makes: 6 servings

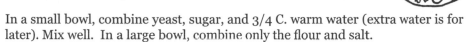

1 1/8 tsp active dry yeast (1/2 sachet)
2 T. white sugar
3/4 C. warm (<u>not</u> hot) water
2 C. all-purpose flour
1 T. baking soda
additional 1 C. warm water
1 T. melted margarine (optional)
1 T. coarse salt (optional)

In a small bowl, combine yeast, sugar, and 3/4 C. warm water (extra water is for later). Mix well. In a large bowl, combine only the flour and salt.

Add liquid mixture to flour mixture and mix well. Dump out onto a lightly floured surface and knead briefly to ensure dry ingredients are fully moistened.

Rinse and grease yer mixing bowl, put dough back into bowl, and turn dough around to coat surface in grease. Cover and let rise fer two hours in a warm area.

After two hours of rising, cut dough into six wedges and roll each into a rope about pencil-thin (it oughta be a couple feet or more in length).

Layer a cookie sheet with parchment paper and combine the extra 1 C. warm water with the baking soda in a shallow bowl or pan.

Tie each dough rope into a pretzel knot like shown above and dip completely in the baking soda water. Place each on the parchment-covered cookie sheet and allow to rise for 20-30 minutes, lightly covered with a towel or plastic wrap.

Preheat oven to 450° F (230° C) and bake for 10 minutes or just until golden brown.

Brush with melted margarine and sprinkle with coarse salt before eatin'!

WHOLEMEAL BREAD

Hearty bread fer toast or sandwiches with fillings like Country-Fried Tofu (p. 81).

prep: 2 hr 55 min | cook: 45 min | makes: 1 loaf

3 1/2 C. wholemeal (whole wheat) flour
1 1/2 tsp. salt
3/4 C. lukewarm water
2 1/4 tsp. active dry yeast (or 1 sachet)
2 T. maple syrup or sugar (white or brown)

In a large bowl, combine flour and salt. In a small bowl, combine the water, yeast, and maple syrup or sugar.

Add liquid to flour mixture and mix well—once it's roughly mixed, dump the contents onto a lightly-floured surface and use yer hands to press and knead it to make sure dry ingredients are completely moistened and all the liquid is absorbed.

Rinse, dry, and grease the large mixing bowl with margarine and place your dough back in it. Cover loosely and leave in a warm spot to rise for two hours.

After two hours, grease a loaf pan with margarine and dump your dough out onto a lightly-floured surface. Fold the dough, shape it into a ball and then stretch it out in one direction to fill the length of yer loaf pan.

Place dough in greased loaf pan and cover with greased plastic wrap or container twice its current height. Let rise in a warm area for 45 minutes.

After 45 minutes, preheat oven to 350° F (175° C). Place loaf pan in center of oven and bake for 45 minutes, until crust is golden brown.

Remove loaf from pan to cool on a rack. If it's stuck, try again 10 minutes later.

CINNAMON RAISIN BREAD

Many a day was started with toast like this as a young 'un and it's still a favorite.

prep: 4 hr 15 min | cook: 45-50 min | makes: 1 loaf

1 1/2 C. soy milk, lukewarm
2 T. margarine, melted
1/4 C. white sugar
2 1/4 tsp. active dry yeast
    (or 1 sachet)
3 1/2 C. all-purpose flour
1 1/2 tsp. cinnamon
1 1/2 tsp. salt
1 C. raisins

In a medium bowl, mix together warm soy milk, melted margarine, sugar, and yeast.

In a large bowl, mix flour, cinnamon, and salt together, then stir raisins throughout.

Mix wet ingredients into the large bowl of flour mixture and mix well until dry ingredients are fully moistened and a dough is formed. Don't be afraid ta get yer hands in there and make sure it's mixed up well, ya don't want any dry pockets hidin' around!

Scrape dough out onto a lightly floured surface and knead a few times with yer hands ta ensure everything is mixed up and distributed well.

Wash out and dry yer large bowl, then grease it lightly with some margarine and place yer dough back in it. Cover with plastic wrap or a large container and leave in a warm area free of drafts to rise for two and a half hours or until twice the size.

After it's risen for the time or size required, grease a loaf pan with a bit of margarine and remove dough from the greased bowl and place back on a lighly floured surface.

Fold dough and shape into a ball. Stretch the ball of dough gently 'til it's about to the length and width of yer loaf pan.

Place the stretched dough inta the greased loaf pan and cover it again. Leave it ta rise yer warm and draft-free area fer another 90 minutes.

Preheat oven to 350° F (175° C) and place yer loaf pan in the center of the oven and bake for 45-50 minutes, until the top has turned a golden brown.

Place loaf pan on a wire rack to cool for 10-15 minutes until bread can be removed from pan. Once removed, leave on wire rack to finish coolin'.

BURGER AND DAWG BUNS

These'll come in handy fer Burgers (p. 70-72), Dawgs (p.86) and Sloppy Joes (p. 79).

prep: 3 hr 30 min | cook: 20 min | makes: 6 buns

1 1/2 C. warm (<u>not</u> hot) water
2 1/4 tsp. active dry yeast
     (or 1 sachet)
2 T. canola oil
1/4 C. white sugar
2 3/4 C. all-purpose flour
3/4 C. whole wheat flour
1 1/2 tsp. salt
sesame seeds (optional)

In a small bowl, combine the water, yeast, and 1 tsp. of sugar.

Reserve 1/2 C. all-purpose flour, then combine remaining flours with salt and remaining sugar in a separate large bowl, stirring well.

Once yeast is fully dissolved in water, add oil to the small bowl and stir it well, then add the liquid ingredients inta yer large bowl of dry ingredients.

Mix well ta moisten dry ingredients and distribute liquid as best ya can. Add as much of the reserved flour needed ta form a dough that ain't stickin' ta everything.

Place dough on a lightly-floured surface and knead it a bit with yer hands to get any pockets of liquid or dry ingredients properly combined so dough is fully moistened.

Grease a large mixing bowl with margarine, and place yer dough in it. Leave the bowl loosely covered in a warm spot to rise fer about two-and-a-half hours or until it's double the size ya left it at.

After yer dough has risen, lightly grease a baking sheet with margarine and dump your dough out onto a lightly-floured surface. Fold the dough, then split it inta six equal-sized chunks and shape them inta balls. If yer after burger buns, squash and stretch the ball gently inta the width of the bun ya want. Fer dawg buns, gently stretch and roll the ball between yer hands inta an oblong shape the length of a bun yer after.

Place the dough on the greased baking sheet, cover loosely and let rise in a warm area for an hour. After an hour, preheat oven to 350° F (175° C).

Brush the tops of the buns with a thin layer of canola oil or melted margarine and sprinkle on some sesame seeds if ya like.

Bake fer 20 minutes, until tops are golden brown.

SAVORY BEER BREAD

Combining two of mah favorite yeast-based goods inta one delicious loaf.

prep: 2 hr 45 min | cook: 45 min | makes: 1 loaf

3/4 C. warm (<u>not</u> hot) water
3/4 C. room temperature beer (see note)
2 1/4 tsp. active dry yeast (1 sachet)
1 T. white sugar
3 C. all-purpose flour
1 1/2 tsp. salt
1/2 yellow onion, finely diced
1 T. canola or olive oil
1/2 tsp. rosemary
1/2 tsp. thyme
1/2 tsp. sage
1/8 tsp. salt
1/8 tsp. black pepper
1/4 tsp. coarse salt

Try an ale or lager for this bread, though a pilsner or kolsch will do if it's all ya got. Darker beers like stouts, porters, and bocks won't taste quite as good.

In a small bowl, combine water, beer, yeast, and white sugar, mixing well.

In a large bowl, combine flour and salt.

Add liquid mixture to flour mixture and mix well ta ensure all dry ingredients are moistened—roll up yer sleeves and get yer hands in there to knead it a bit if need be.

Cover bowl with a towel or plastic wrap and leave in a warm area to rise for two hours.

After an hour, heat oil in a small skillet over medium-high heat. Add onions and quickly break up to spread out and stir well before reducing heat to medium.

Add <u>half</u> of the rosemary, thyme, and sage into the skillet (the rest is for garnish) along with salt and pepper and sauté until onions are softened but not browned.

Remove from heat and set aside to cool while bread finishes the initial rise.

After two hours, remove bread from bowl and fold on a lightly floured surface, then gently stretch out into a flat square surface one to two feet wide.

Spread onion and herb mixture on to bread and fold again to layer throughout.

(continued on next page)

(Savory Beer Bread, continued)

Grease and flour a loaf pan. Shape the dough into a ball then gently stretch it in one direction ta form a loaf ta fill the length of yer pan. Some of the onions will more'n likely work their way out, but poke 'em right back in and pinch over to cover.

Set dough into loaf pan and cover. Allow to rise for another 45 minutes.

After 30 minutes, preheat oven to 400° F (200° C) so it's ready to go.

When oven is preheated and bread has risen, brush the top with water using a pastry brush (or a dripping wet paper towel works in a pinch) and sprinkle with the reserved 1/4 teaspoons of rosemary, thyme, and sage as well as coarse salt. Use a serrated knife to cut a line down center of loaf about 1/4-inch (1/2 cm) deep.

Bake for 45 minutes; it'll be dark brown and make yer mouth start ta water!

CINNAMON ROLLS

I don't reckon ya need an introduction to these particular delicious treats, do ya?

prep: 3 hr 50 min | cook: 25 min | makes: 10-12 servings

1/2 C. warm (<u>not</u> hot) water
2 1/4 tsp. active dry yeast (1 sachet)
1/2 C. warm soy milk
1 C. margarine, melted and divided
1 1/4 C. white sugar, divided
1 tsp. salt
1/4 C. silken tofu, squeezed, drained and
  mashed well or pureed
3 1/2 C. all-purpose flour
1 T. cinnamon
1/2 C. raisins (optional)
1/2 C. walnuts, chopped (optional)
2 C. powdered sugar
3 T. warm water
1 tsp. vanilla extract
1/2 tsp. maple syrup (optional)

In a small bowl, combine 1/2 C. warm water, yeast, and 1 tsp. sugar. Mix well and set aside.

In a large bowl, combine warm soy milk, 1/3 C. melted margarine, 1/3 C. sugar, salt, and tofu. Stir together and then add yer yeast liquid, mixin' well to combine.

Add 2 C. flour and mix well, and add remaining flour 1/2 C. at a time, mixing well until ya get a fairly stiff dough (you'll probably want ta use yer hands around then).

Use remaining flour to dust a flat surface for kneading, then turn the dough out onta that surface and knead until the remaining flour is combined as best ya kin get it. Yer goal is more to incorporate the flour than ta get gluten strands formin' at this point.

Wash out and grease yer large mixing bowl with extra margarine, then place the dough in it and leave covered in a warm place for 2 1/2 hours, until double the size.

Turn the dough out onto a lightly-floured surface, then stretch it out and press it down before rolling it out into a rectangle 1/2-inch thick.

Brush dough with 2 T. melted margarine, then mix together 1/2 C. sugar with the 1 T. cinnamon and sprinkle all over the dough, right up ta the edges. If ya want ta add the raisins and walnuts, now's the time—sprinkle them evenly over the dough as well.

(continued on next page)

(Cinnamon Rolls, continued)

Reserve 1/3 C. melted margarine and use the rest to coat the bottom of an 9 x 13 (33 x 23 cm) baking pan, then sprinkle the pan with yer remaining white sugar.

Roll up the dough along the longest side and seal the last edge by pinchin' it firmly with the rolled dough it's in contact with. Cut into 10-12 even rolls and place 'em cut-side down close ta each other in the greased baking pan.

Cover the pan and place in a warm spot to let the rolls rise another 45 minutes.

Preheat the oven to 350° F (175° C), then bake the rolls 20-25 minutes, 'til they're golden brown and the smell's drivin' ya crazy—take 'em out and let 'em start ta cool.

In a medium bowl, mix the reserved 1/3 melted margarine, powdered sugar, vanilla extract, and maple syrup well. Add warm water 1 T. at a time, mixing well after each addition until the icing is as thick or thin as ya'd like it.

Spread the icing over the rolls and start devouring 'em!

PECAN STICKY BUNS

If Cinnamon Rolls make yer day, wait 'til ya try one of these ta greet the sunrise!

prep: 2 hr 55 min | cook: 45 min | makes: 10-12 servings

9 x 13 inch baking pan (22 x 33 cm)
baking sheet
parchment paper or aluminium foil
2 1/4 C. all-purpose flour
1/4 C. white sugar
2 1/4 tsp. active dry yeast (1 sachet)
1 tsp. salt
2 T. margarine
1/4 C. silken tofu, squeezed, drained, and
 mashed well or pureed
3/4 C. warm (not hot) soy milk

In a large bowl, combine 1 1/2 C. flour, sugar, yeast, and salt, mixing thoroughly.

In a medium bowl, cream together margarine and tofu, then add in the warm soy milk and combine this all with the large bowl of dry ingredients and mix well.

Begin adding the remaining flour, 1/4 C. at a time, stirring until ya can't stir any more flour in but you've got a dough you can handle. Dust a clean work surface with the remaining flour and turn out your dough onto it, kneading to incorporate all the flour ya got left and adding any more as needed ta get a smooth dough that ain't sticky.

Place the dough back in yer large bowl and leave covered with a dishtowel or lightly covered with plastic wrap in a warm spot for 2 1/2 hours or until doubled in size.

After dough has risen, prepare a 9 x 13 inch (22 x 33 cm) baking pan by combining the following in a small saucepan and heating over medium heat until simmering:

3 T. margarine
1/3 C. brown sugar
2 T. corn syrup
1 tsp. vanilla

Allow it ta simmer fer a few minutes, then pour it inta the pan, and sprinkle with:

3/4 C. pecans, chopped

(continued on next page)

47

(Pecan Sticky Buns, continued)

With yer pan prepared, now you'll wanta combine in a small bowl:

1/4 C. margarine
1/2 C. brown sugar

Take yer dough out of the bowl and roll it out on a lightly-floured surface inta a square about 12 inches (30 1/2 cm) wide and spread the brown sugar mixture evenly on it. Don't skimp anywhere, spread it right on up to the edges!

Start at one edge and roll the dough tightly inta a long, doughy tube, then slice inta 10 or 12 slices about 1 inch (2 1/4 cm) wide and place facing down in yer pan.

Cover the buns with a dishtowel or loosely with plastic wrap and allow ta rise for 45 minutes to an hour, until doubled in size, or crowding one another on the pan.

Preheat oven to 350° F (175° C). Brush the tops of the buns lightly with oil or melted margarine and place the pan in the center of yer oven.

Bake for 45 minutes. They oughta be turning golden brown by about then.

Remove the pan from the oven and set it aside ta cool for five to ten minutes.

Cover the baking sheet with parchament paper or aluminum foil, then place it upside-down on top of the baking pan (so the paper or foil is facing the buns—ya probably see what we're about ta do here).

Using potholders or dishtowels ta keep yer hands from burning, clamp the baking pan and baking sheet together with yer hands and flip the whole thing over so the baking pan is now upside-down on top of the baking sheet.

Lift the baking pan off and ya oughta be greeted with the side of yer sticky buns topped with pecans and covered in a delicious caramel-like sauce.

Serve warm, but enjoy one a' these straight away—you've earned it, pardner!

SIDE DISHES

REFRIED BEANS

You'll find these handy fer Nachos (p.76) and Enchiladas (p. 77), just fer starters.

prep: 2 min | cook: 30 min | makes: 6 servings

3 C. beans (kidney, black, or pinto), cooked and drained
1 1/2 C. water
1 T. dried minced onion
1/2 tsp. salt
extra water

Combine all ingredients in a medium-sized saucepan and bring to a boil over medium-high heat. Lower heat and simmer about ten minutes, until the cooked beans soften. Mash beans and return to a simmer for another 15-20 minutes, until liquid reduces and beans thicken. Stir frequently to prevent scorchin' on bottom of pan.

SPANISH RICE

Use this in yer Enchiladas (p. 77), or next ta Fajitas (p. 76), and Burritos (pgs. 73, 74).

prep: 5 min | cook: 25 min | makes: 6 servings

3 C. white rice, cooked
1 onion, chopped
1 green bell pepper, chopped
2 T. canola oil
1 stalk celery, finely chopped
1 can chopped tomatoes
1 tsp. paprika
1/2 t. cumin
1/8 tsp. black pepper
1/8 tsp. salt
1/2 tsp. oregano
1/8 tsp cayenne pepper
1/2 C. water

Heat oil in a skillet over medium-high heat and sauté onion a few minutes until it's translucent. Add bell pepper, celery, and spices, and cook fer another five minutes.

Add chopped tomatoes, cooked rice, and water—it oughta have a soupy consistency.

Simmer until it reduces and thickens, stirring occasionally to ensure flavors mix and it ain't scorchin'. Add extra spices before servin' if it ain't quite ta yer taste

RED BEANS AND RICE

A good n' spicy dish to accompany Hush Puppies (p.15) or Cornbread (p.14).

prep: 15 min | cook: 55 min | makes: 8 servings

3 C. white rice, cooked
1 1/2 C. kidney beans, cooked and drained
1 1/2 C/ chopped tomatoes with juice.
1/4 C. celery, finely chopped
1/2 green bell pepper, chopped
1-2 T. chili powder (to taste)
1 1/2 T. beef-style broth powder
2 tsp. minced onion
2 tsp. Worcestershire Sauce (p. 12)
2 tsp. brown sugar
1 tsp. Tabasco sauce
1 tsp. Cajun Spice Mix (p. 20)
1/2 tsp. cayenne pepper
1/2 tsp. minced garlic
1/4 tsp. paprika
1/8 tsp. dried marjoram
1/8 tsp. dried oregano
1 bay leaf

Mix everything together in a large pot, and add just enough water to reach the top of yer ingredients. Stir well so spices mix and both the broth powder and sugar dissolve.

Bring to a boil over medium heat, stirring to keep from scorching. Reduce heat and simmer uncovered 30-45 minutes, stirring frequently to prevent scorchin' until the liquid reduces and contents thicken. Remove the bay leaf before servin'.

BLACK BEANS AND RICE

An alternative to the previous cajun variety, but just as tasty, I assure ya.
prep: 10 min | cook: 35 min | makes: 6-8 servings

1 T. canola oil
1 onion, chopped
2 cloves garlic, minced
1 jalapeno pepper, seeded, de-veined and chopped
1 1/2 C. black beans, cooked and drained
1 1/2 C. white rice, cooked
1 1/2 C. vegetable broth
1 1/2 C. diced tomatoes
1 1/2 C. corn (thaw if frozen)
1 tsp. oregano
1 tsp. cumin
1/2 tsp. paprika
1/4 tsp. cayenne pepper

Heat oil in a large pot over medium high heat, and sauté onion, garlic, and jalapeno a few minutes until they've begun to soften but not brown.

Add the rice and cook another couple minutes before adding all of the remaining ingredients and stirring well.

Bring to a boil, then cover with the lid ajar and reduce the heat to a simmer. Be sure ta stir occasionally ta ensure there's no scorchin' on the bottom of the pot.

Simmer for 20-25 minutes, until most of the liquid is reduced and absorbed.

BAKED BEANS
A shortcut version for the spicy sweet beans that no picnic oughta do without

prep: 18 min | cook: 1hr 30min | makes: 4-6 servings

3 C. kidney, pinto or navy beans, cooked and drained
1 onion, diced fine
1/4 C. brown sugar
1/2 C. tomato sauce or ketchup
2 T. molasses
1 T. Worchestershire Sauce (p. 12)
1 tsp. salt
1/4 tsp. black pepper
1/2 tsp. mustard powder
1/2 C. vegetable broth or water

In a large saucepan or medium-sized stockpot, bring the broth or water to a simmer and add the diced onion, simmering fer a few minutes to soften it up.

Add the remaining ingredients and mix well. Heat to a boil, then reduce heat and simmer it with the lid ajar fer at least 30 minutes, or 45 minutes ta get softer beans.

As ya near the 30-minute mark, preheat your oven to 325° F (165° C) and take the lid off the beans on the stove. If ya reckon the sauce has reduced more than you'd like, stir in another 1/4 C. water and mix well, there's still some cookin' yet ta go!

Now that you've got yer oven pre-heated and yer beans pre-cooked, pour all that simmerin' goodness into an 8-inch (20 cm) square non-metal baking dish.

Cover your baking dish with aluminium foil and/or a lid and bake for 45 minutes.

Serve warm, hopefully accompanied by coleslaw (p. 53) and potato salad (p. 54)!

ROASTED GARLIC AND HERB COUSCOUS

It's quick n' easy and it tastes mighty fine—make sure ta use fresh garlic.

prep: 10 min | makes: 6 servings

1 1/4 C. vegetable broth
1/2 tsp. salt
1 C. dry couscous
2 cloves garlic, minced
2 T. olive oil
1/4 tsp. black pepper
1/2 tsp. thyme
1/2 tsp. dried basil
1/2 tsp. paprika

Bring vegetable broth to a boil, then add salt and couscous; remove from heat and leave covered for 10 minutes.

Heat oil in a small saucepan over medium heat and cook garlic just until it begins to brown. Add spices and stir, cooking another 30 seconds before removing from heat.

Fluff the couscous with a fork, then add the roasted garlic and herbs (along with oil), and stir well to mix the flavors throughout. Serve warm.

COLESLAW

Great with yer usual picnic eats like burgers (pgs. 70-72) and Dawgs (p. 86), plus chilis (pgs. 65-67) or next ta Red Beans and Rice (p.50) and Hush Puppies (p. 25).

prep: 15 min | makes: 6-8 servings

1 head green cabbage, shredded or finely chopped
2 medium carrots, shredded or finely chopped
3/4 C. soy mayonnaise (p. 18)
1/4 C.soy milk mixed with 1 tsp. lemon juice
2 T. white vinegar
1 T. lemon juice
2 T. white sugar
1 tsp. salt
1/4 tsp. black pepper

Toss cabbage and carrots in a large bowl. Mix well. In a medium bowl, mix remaining ingredients well. Add to the large bowl.

Toss well to mix liquid throughout. Refrigerate an hour or more to chill, and toss again before serving to mix liquid that'll settles down in the bottom of yer bowl.

POTATO SALAD

Great alongside Burgers (pgs. 71-72), Dawgs (p. 86), and Country-Fried Tofu (p. 81).

prep: 10 min | makes: 6 servings

4 C. potatoes, chopped, steamed, and cooled
1/2 C. celery, chopped
1/3 C. pickles, chopped
1/4 C. red onion, finely chopped
1/4 C. green onions, sliced
1/2 C. red bell pepper, chopped
2 T. parsley, finely chopped
1/2 C. soy mayonnaise (p. 11)
1-2 T. prepared American mustard
1/2 tsp. black pepper
1/4 tsp. salt

In a medium bowl, combine all ingredients except the potatoes and mix well.

Add the potatoes and toss well to coat; easy! Refrigerate before serving.

GARLIC MASHED POTATOES

Slap these down next ta Country-Fried Tofu (p. 81) and fill on up!

prep: 5 min + 5 min | cook: 20 min | makes: 4-6 servings

3 large potatoes, cubed (peeling optional)
5 C. broth, vegetable or beef-style
3 garlic cloves, minced
3 T. margarine
black pepper (to taste)
salt (to taste)
1-2 T. soy milk (optional)

In a pot over medium-high heat, bring broth, potatoes and garlic to a boil.

Reduce heat to medium and cover, cooking until potatoes are soft (10-15 minutes).

Drain potatoes, reserving 1/2 C. of the broth and keeping the garlic with the taters.

In a large bowl, mash the potatoes and garlic with the margarine, salt and pepper.

Add reserved broth a bit at a time, until potatoes are mashed to the consistency yer after. If you've got soy milk handy and want a creamier texture, try mixin' a couple tablespoons of that in as well.

HOME FRIES

A breakfast staple in any southern diner or breakfast nook.
Serve along with Biscuits and Gravy (p. 81) and Breakfast Links (p. 90).
prep: 5 min | cook: 15 min | makes: 4-6 servings

3 C. potatoes, cubed and baked/steamed
1 red bell pepper, diced
1 onion, chopped
3 T. canola oil
1/2 tsp. paprika
1/2 tsp. parsley
1/2 tsp. sage
1/2 tsp. salt
1/2 tsp. black pepper

Hcat 1 T. of oil in a large skillet over medium-high heat and sauté the onion and bell pepper until it begins to soften, about 3 minutes. Remove the cooked pepper and onions from yer skillet and set aside on a plate or in a medium-sized bowl fer later.

Add remaining 2 T. of oil to the skillet and return it to the stove, still on medium-high heat. Add potatoes and spread out into a single layer, then mash down slightly with yer cooking utensil.

Leave for about two minutes until starting to brown and then flip the potatoes over and do the same for the other side. Repeat the process once more and then add the onions and peppers back into the skillet and mix well.

Continue cooking another five to six minutes, allowing contents to cook in place a minute or more before stirring again. Remove from heat when onions start to brown and serve hot (or warm if you can stand ta let 'em cool).

TWICE-BAKED TATERS
I'd be lyin' if I said I hadn't just eaten these as a meal themselves at times!

prep: 20 min | cook: 1hr 15 min | makes: 8 servings

4 large baking potatoes (Russet variety if possible)
1 C. Almost Sour Cream (p. 17)
1 C. Cheese Sauce (p. 12, about 1/2 recipe)
4 T. margarine
1/2 tsp. salt
1/2 tsp. black pepper
1 C. green onion, chopped

Wash yer potatoes and jab vents in 'em with a fork while preheating the oven to 350° F (175° C). Place taters in preheated oven and cook until done, about 1 hour.

Let the taters cool enough ta handle, then cut them in half lengthwise to get ya two long halves ta work with. Carefully scoop out the baked insides with a spoon, but leave about 1/4 inch (2/3 cm) of potato at the edges.

Place baked tater scrapings in a medium-sized bowl and add the Almost Sour Cream, 1/2 C. of the Cheese Sauce, margarine, salt and pepper, and mix it until well-blended.

Preheat yer oven back to 350° F (175° C).

Place yer scooped-out baked tater halves on a cookie sheet, then divide the tasty tater filling between each of them and press it down gently ta pack it in.

Top each half with with the remaining Cheese Sauce and chopped green onions, then bake them in the preheated oven for an additional 15 minutes. Serve warm!

FRIED JALAPENO POPPERS

Great alongside Burgers (pgs. 70-72), Dawgs (p. 86), and Country-Fried Tofu (p. 81).
prep: 30 min | cook: 18 min | makes: 6 servings

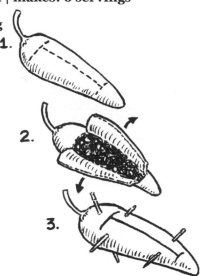

Deep fryer or deep saucepan for frying
1 quart canola oil for deep-frying
6 fresh jalapeno peppers
1/2 C. filling of yer choice; try:
 - Cheese Sauce
 - Spanish Rice
 - Taco and Burrito Fill
 and try combinin' some together
18 toothpicks
1/2 C. all-purpose flour
1/2 C. cornmeal
2 T. C. white sugar
1/4 tsp. salt
a dash of black pepper
1 tsp. baking powder
1/2 C. soy milk

I highly advise wearin' food-preparation gloves when seeding these puppies ta avoid rubbin' yer eyes or other sensitives with pepper juice soaked inta yer hands!

In a medium-sized saucepan, bring 6 C. water and a dash of salt to a boil. Blanch the jalapenos in the boiling water for three minutes, then place in a bowl of cold water to cool them down a few minutes.

Pat the jalapenos dry, and with a sharp knife, carefully cut an "I"-shaped cut inta them about a fingers-width below the stem and no more than a 1/3 through the pepper as pictured above. Carefully hold those flaps open with one hand and scrape out the seeds and ribs; flush the pepper out with cold water ta ensure ya got 'em all.

With all the peppers seeded, fill them with about a tablespoon of yer filling of choice, and use the toothpicks through the sides ta pin the flaps together at top and bottom and one from the front of the stem through the back of the pepper ta keep it together.

With that done, get yer oil heating to 375° F (190° C) in yer deep-fryer or pan. In a medium-sized bowl, mix together the flour, cornmeal, sugar, salt, pepper, baking powder, and soy milk. Add 1-2 T. extra soy milk if it's too thick for you ta work with.

Holding the peppers by their stems, gently dip each of them into the bowl and spoon the batter overtop and around the peppers ta ensure they're completely covered.

Fry for three to five minutes in the heated oil, until browned ta yer liking'—serve hot!

SPICY PEANUTS

Great ta munch on while yer killin' time before a proper meal

prep: 3 min | cook: 5 min | makes: 1 C.

1 C. unsalted peanuts, shelled and without skins
3-5 garlic cloves, halved lengthwise
1 1/2 tsp. canola oil
1 tsp. chili powder
1 tsp. oregano
1/2-1 tsp. salt (to taste)
1/2 tsp. onion powder
1/4 tsp. cumin
1/8 tsp. black pepper

Set a medium heatproof bowl aside. In a small bowl or saucer, mix spices together.

Heat oil in a skillet over medium-high heat. Once heated, add garlic and peanuts.

Cook for three to five minutes until peanuts begin to brown but not char—stir and shake the skillet constantly to prevent peanuts from scorching.

Remove skillet from heat and scoop nuts and garlic into the medium heatproof bowl (avoid dumping leftover oil in with 'em). Add mixed spices and toss well to coat.

Serve warm or store in an airtight container once cooled for snackin' on later.

SPICED PECANS

Spicy pecans fer a bit more elaborate snackin' than peanuts

prep: 8 min | cook: 20 min | makes: 1 C.

1 C. pecans
1 1/4 tsp. Worchestershire Sauce (p. 12)
1 tsp. canola oil
1/2 tsp. ground coriander
1/2 tsp. cumin
1/4 tsp. chili powder
1/4 tsp. salt (or to taste)
1/8 tsp. cardamom (optional)
dash cayenne pepper

Preheat oven to 300° F (150° C) and line a cookie sheet with aluminium foil.

In a small bowl, whisk all ingredients except salt together well.

Put pecans in a medium bowl, pour liquid over 'em and toss well to fully cover.

Spread pecans evenly on the foil-lined cookie sheet and sprinkle with salt.

Bake for twenty minutes in preheated oven, until nuts are darker brown and dry.

Store in an airtight container ta keep fresh until served.

SOUPS AND CHILIS

Soups and chilis—along with bread and biscuits—are always mah preferred go-to come wintertime! Cookin' up a great big, steaming pot of vegetables and spices gets the house smellin' great, brings a bit of welcome heat into the bones and fills up the freezer for hearty eatin' for lunch or dinner all week.

GARLIC SOUP

This'll cure what ails ya! If it doesn't at least get yer nose running,
well ah got some bad news—there's no hope for ya, pardner!

prep: 18 min | cook: 45 min | makes: 4-6 servings

8 C. water
1 large onion, chopped
2 bulbs of garlic cloves, separated and peeled
2 stalks celery, chopped
2 carrots, chopped
4 large potatoes, cubed
2 C. cabbage, chopped (optional)
1 C. corn kernels (optional)
1 tsp. salt
1 tsp. cracked black pepper
1/2 tsp. cayenne pepper

Bring water to boil in a large pot, then add the onion, garlic, celery, and carrots. Cook five to ten minutes then add yer remaining ingredients and return to a boil.

Reduce heat and simmer for 20-30 more minutes, stirring occasionally. Top up with water to cover contents if it's becomin' too thick for yer liking.

Best pureed (or at least mashed) so it's only slightly chunky before serving.

CLASSIC VEGETABLE SOUP
A chunky vegetable soup ta warm ya up on those cold days and nights.
prep: 12 min | cook: 50 min | makes: 6-8 servings

4 C. water
2 C. vegetable broth
3 C. diced tomatoes with juice
1 onion, chopped
1 large potato, cubed
2 carrots, sliced
2 stalks celery, sliced
1 C. green beans
1 C. corn kernels
1/2 tsp. salt
1/2 tsp. black pepper
1/2 tsp. garlic powder

If ya'd like to freeze this for eatin' in the longer term, ya kin get more mileage outta it by mixing in 1/2 C. tomato paste at the end of cooking. It'll thicken up somethin' fierce, so use a smaller servin' size then add water ta fill up the rest of yer bowl and mix to thin out ta normal consistency—works like charm!

Combine all ingredients in a large pot and bring to a boil.

Once boiling, reduce heat to simmer for 30 minutes, until vegetables are tender.

Try topping with fresh-cracked pepper ta help clear out them sinuses when eatin'!

61

PUMPKIN SOUP

If ya got a bit of pumpkin on hand, try whippin' up this soup on a cold winter day.
prep: 25 min | cook: 35 min | makes: 4-6 servings

4 C. fresh pumpkin, chopped
1 C. cauliflower, chopped
1 red bell pepper, chopped
1 onion, chopped
2 T. vegetable oil
2 T. fresh ginger, chopped
2 C. chicken-style broth
1 1/2 C. coconut milk
1 tsp. chili pepper, chopped
1 T. lemon juice
1 T. tomato paste
1/8 tsp. sugar
1/4 tsp. fresh cracked black pepper
salt to taste
2 T. cilantro (garnish)

In a large pot, sauté pumpkin, capsicum, onion, and cauliflower in oil over medium heat for about five minutes.

Add ginger, water, and broth. Bring to a boil, then reduce heat and simmer for 15 minutes. Add rest of ingredients except cilantro and return to a boil for five minutes.

Mash well or puree soup in a blender if ya like it smooth, and serve garnished with a bit of cilantro and a slice of some fresh, toasted wholemeal bread (p. 40).

BLACK BEAN SOUP

A nice and easy l'il soup ta enjoy with some biscuits (pgs. 26, 32, 33).

prep: 10 min | cook: 1 hr 15 min | makes: 4 servings

1 T. canola oil
1 medium onion, chopped
2 cloves garlic, minced
1 carrot, sliced
1 celery stalk, sliced
1 red bell pepper, chopped.
1 bay leaf
1/4 tsp. thyme
1/2 tsp. chili powder
1/4 tsp. cayenne pepper
1/4 tsp. black pepper
1/4 tsp. salt
1 tsp. white sugar
1 tsp. red wine vinegar
3 C. black beans, cooked and drained
4 C. vegetable broth
fresh parsley or sliced green onions (garnish)

Heat the oil in a large pot over medium-high heat and sauté the onion and garlic a few minutes, until onion begins to soften but not brown.

Add remaining vegetables and cook until they begin to soften as well, 3-5 minutes.

Add remaining ingredients and mix well, then cover and bring to a boil.

Once boiling, reduce heat and simmer covered for one hour, stirring occasionally ta prevent anything from scorchin' to the bottom of yer pot.

Top up with additional water if ya reckon it's becoming too thick for yer likin'.

Serve garnished with fresh parsley sprigs or sliced green onions.

VEGETABLE MINESTRONE

Why settle fer minestrone outta some can when ya kin make better on yer own?

prep: 22 min | cook: 50 min | makes: 6-8 servings

2 T. olive oil
1 onion, chopped
1 clove garlic, minced
1 C. carrots, sliced
1 C. celery, chopped
1 C. chicken-style broth
4 C. water
1 C. tomato paste
1 1/2 C. kidney beans, cooked and drained
1 C. green beans
2 C. spinach, chopped
1 C. zucchini, chopped
2 T. oregano
1 T. basil
1/2 tsp. salt
1/2 tsp. pepper
1 C. rollini pasta, uncooked

In a large pot, heat olive oil over medium-high heat. Sauté onion and garlic until onion becomes translucent. Add carrots and celery and sauté a few minutes more.

Add broth, water, and tomato paste. Mix well and bring to a boil, stirring frequently. Add remaining ingredients except pasta and reduce heat to a simmer.

Simmer fer 35-45 minutes, stirring occasionally and topping off with water to keep from reducing too much.

At about the 30 minute mark, cook the rollini pasta in a separate pot and drain. Stir cooked pasta inta hot soup just before serving. Garnish with parsley or cilantro.

VEGETABLE CHILI

Dang near the best chili I've ever made—serve it up with Cornbread (p.24)!

prep: 22 min | cook: 50 min | makes: 6-8 servings

3 T. olive oil
1 medium onion, chopped
4 cloves garlic, minced
1 C. chopped mushrooms
2 C. chopped cauliflower pieces
3 C. corn kernels
1 large potato, peeled and cubed
2 carrots, chopped
1 green bell pepper, chopped
3 C. kidney beans, cooked and drained
1 can chopped tomatoes with juice
1 C. tomato juice or puree
2 T. chili powder
1 tsp. paprika
1 T. cumin
1/8 tsp. cayenne pepper
2 T. tomato paste
3 T. red wine vinegar

Heat oil in a large pot over medium heat. Sauté onions and garlic until onion is translucent, then add the mushrooms and sauté another four to six minutes.

Stir in the rest of the ingredients one at a time and mix well after each addition.

Bring the entire mixture to a boil, then reduce heat and simmer covered for about 30 minutes, stirring occasionally to prevent scorching on the bottom. Serve hot!

BLACK BEAN CHILI

A different chili than the previous variety, but still good with Cornbread (p.24)!

prep: 10 min | cook: 50 min | makes: 4 servings

1 T. canola oil
1 onion, chopped
3 cloves garlic, minced
1 green bell pepper, chopped
3 C. black beans, cooked and drained
3 C. diced tomatoes with juice
1 C. water
1-3 T. chili powder (to taste)
1 tsp. ground cumin
1/2 tsp. dried oregano
1/2 tsp. ground cinnamon
1/2 tsp. brown sugar
1/4 tsp. salt
1/4 tsp. black pepper
chopped green onions or cilantro (garnish)

Heat oil in a large pot over medium-high heat.

Add the onion, garlic, and bell pepper, then sauté until onion is translucent.

Stir in the chili powder, cumin, oregano, and cinnamon, cooking until well-mixed and liquid is absorbed by the spices.

Add the diced tomatoes and water, then bring to a boil, stirring occasionally to prevent scorching on the bottom of the pot. Add beans, sugar, salt, and pepper.

Stir well and return it to a boil. Reduce heat and simmer for 30 minutes, stirring to prevent any scorchin'. Garnish with green onions or cilantro before serving.

CAMPFIRE CHILI

A thick and hearty chili like ya'd be hopin' ta see in a pot hangin'
over the fire when ya head inta camp after a long day on the trail.

prep: 7 min | cook: 1hr 15 min | makes: 6-8 servings

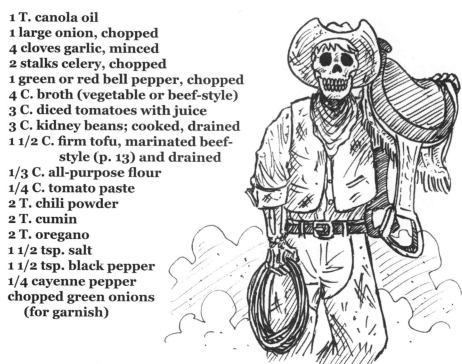

1 T. canola oil
1 large onion, chopped
4 cloves garlic, minced
2 stalks celery, chopped
1 green or red bell pepper, chopped
4 C. broth (vegetable or beef-style)
3 C. diced tomatoes with juice
3 C. kidney beans; cooked, drained
1 1/2 C. firm tofu, marinated beef-
     style (p. 13) and drained
1/3 C. all-purpose flour
1/4 C. tomato paste
2 T. chili powder
2 T. cumin
2 T. oregano
1 1/2 tsp. salt
1 1/2 tsp. black pepper
1/4 cayenne pepper
chopped green onions
    (for garnish)

Mix flour, 1 tsp. salt and 1 tsp. pepper together in a bowl and set aside. Heat oil in a large pot over medium-high heat. Sauté onion, bell pepper and celery until softened.

Add remaining spices and continue cooking another few minutes, mixing well.

Add broth, tomatoes, and beans, stirring well. Bring to a boil and then reduce heat to medium and simmer for 30 minutes, stirring often to prevent scorching.

After 30 minutes, toss marinated tofu with the flour and spice mix, coating the tofu.

Add yer now-coated tofu and any straggling spiced flour into the stew pot and allow to simmer another 30 minutes, still stirring often to avoid scorching on the bottom.

Remove from heat and try topping with Almost Sour Cream (p. 17) and/or Cheese Sauce (p. 12) along with the chopped green onions fer garnish and a Classic Drop Biscuit (p. 32) or some Cornbread (p. 24) on th' side! Hot damn that's good eatin'!

CHILI CON NON-CARNE

Another type a' chili—the original variety was just meat an' spices, but I wrangled it 'round ta accommodate mah slightly different tastes. Try with Cornbread (p.24).

prep:10 min | cook: 40 min | makes: 4-6 servings

1 C. TVP granules, dry
1 C. hot water
2 T. vegetable oil
1 onion, chopped
2 cloves garlic, chopped
3 C. chopped tomatoes and juice
1 1/2 C. kidney beans, cooked and drained
1/2 tsp. salt
1/2 tsp. black pepper
3 tsp. ground cumin
1 tsp. chili powder
1 T. paprika
1 T. dried oregano
1 cinnamon stick
3 whole cloves
1 C. frozen corn kernels (optional)

Combine TVP granules with hot water in a small bowl and set aside. If usin' frozen corn kernels, set 'em aside to thaw a bit (unless it's fresh corn, then yer good ta go).

Heat oil in a medium-sized pot over medium-high heat. Sauté the onion and garlic until soft, then add the rehydrated TVP, tomatoes, and spices.

Cover and allow to simmer 30 minutes, stirring occasionally. Stir in beans and the optional corn kernels if you've gone that route, and cook until heated through.

Remove whole cloves and the cinnamon stick before servin'.

SOUTHWESTERN PRARIE SOUP
A filling soup with a hint of heat, beggin' ta be eaten with drop biscuits (pgs. 32, 33).

prep:10 min | cook: 45 min | makes: 4-6 servings

2 C. firm or extra firm tofu, marinated
 chicken-style and drained well
3 T. canola oil
1 medium onion, chopped
2 cloves garlic, minced
1 red bell pepper, chopped
1 large potato, cubed
1 jalapeno pepper, seeded and minced
1 1/2 C. black or kidney beans,
       cooked and drained
1 C. corn kernels (frozen or fresh)
5 C. vegetable or chicken-flavor broth
1/2 tsp. sage
1/2 tsp. oregano
1/2 tsp. salt
1/4 tsp. black pepper
1/4 tsp. cayenne pepper
1/4 C. green onions, chopped (for garnish)

Heat 2 T. oil in a medium-sized pot over medium-high heat and cook tofu until browned all over, 10-12 minutes. Transfer to a bowl or plate and set aside fer later.

Heat remaining 1 T. oil in pot and add onion and garlic. Sauté until onion begins to wilt but not brown, about three minutes.

Add red bell pepper and sauté another few minutes until pepper begins to soften.

Add remaining ingredients including tofu and bring to a boil.

Reduce heat to a simmer and cook for another fifteen minutes until potatoes are tender and soup has begun to thicken.

Garnish with chopped green onions and dig in!

MAIN DISHES

LENTIL BURGERS

Lentil burgers are one of the easiest and tastiest bean burgers ya kin make. Have 'em on toasted homemade Burger Buns (p. 42) with all the usual fixins, and a side of Coleslaw (p. 53) and/or Potato Salad (p. 54) and see if ya don't go fer another.

prep: 50 min | cook: 12 min | makes: 6 servings

1 1/2 C. dry lentils
1 bay leaf
1 onion, finely diced
2 cloves garlic, crushed
3 T. tomato sauce or ketchup
2 T. peanut butter
1 T. olive oil
1/2 tsp. thyme
1/2 tsp. parsley
1/8 tsp. black pepper
dash of salt
dash of Tabasco sauce (optional)
1 C. dry bread crumbs
1/4 C. all-purpose flour

Cover lentils with water in a saucepan and simmer with the bay leaf for about 30 minutes. Once cooked, drain the lentils well and chuck out the bay leaf.

Heat the olive oil in a saucepan or skillet over medium heat. Sauté the onion and garlic in the oil for a couple minutes, then add the rest of yer ingredients except the breadcrumbs in a bowl and mash well, or use a food processor/blender if ya like.

Stir bread crumbs and mashed/blended mixture well in a large bowl—it'll still be pretty moist but should stick together plenty fine. Form inta patties and dust with a bit of all-purpose flour to help keep 'em from stickin' to everything.

Cook on medium-high heat in a lightly oiled skillet until browned and firm in center.

BLACK BEAN BURGERS

Spicy bean burgers askin' ta be topped with Cheese Sauce (p. 12), Salsa (p. 15),
Guacamole (p. 17), Almost Sour Cream (p. 17) or any other Tex-Mex fixins ya like.

prep: 13 + 15 min | cook: 13 + 22 min | makes: 9 servings

1 T. canola oil
1 small onion, chopped
1/2 red bell pepper, chopped
1 carrot, shredded
1 C. fresh tomato, seeded and chopped
1/4 C. fresh cilantro, chopped (optional)
1 tsp. dried oregano
1 tsp. chili powder
1 tsp. garlic powder
1/2 tsp. sugar
1/2 tsp. cumin
1/2 tsp. paprika
1/4 tsp. black pepper
1/8 tsp. salt
1 1/2 C. white rice, cooked
    (or 1/2 C. uncooked)
3 C. black beans, cooked
    and drained
1/2 C. corn kernels, cooked
1 C. bread crumbs
1 C. flour (optional, for dredging)

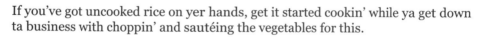

If you've got uncooked rice on yer hands, get it started cookin' while ya get down ta business with choppin' and sautéing the vegetables for this.

Heat oil in a skillet over medium-high heat and sauté onion until translucent.

Add bell pepper, tomato, cilantro, carrot, and spices, sautéing 'til tender (~5 min).

In a large bowl, combine sautéed vegetables with corn, beans, and cooked rice.

Mix and mash it well, then add the bread crumbs to the bowl and mix well with yer hands, until bread crumbs are distributed throughout, and the mix holds together well.

Form the mix inta patties and dust lightly with flour if ya'd like to keep 'em from stickin' to their resting place before cooking (ya kin also try parchment paper).

Cook patties in a lightly oiled skillet over medium-high heat until cooked through and browned on both sides.

Serve on toasted buns (p. 42) with yer favorite tex-mex toppings of choice.

CLASSIC BURGERS

Juicy, tangy burgers fit fer a barbeque, picnic, or just a night on the grill.

prep: 15 min | cook: 15 min | makes: 6-8 servings

2 C. (350g) firm/extra-firm tofu, marinated
beef-style (p. 13), well-drained and crumbled
3/4 C. quick-cooking oats (uncooked)
1/2 C. all-purpose flour
1/4 C. tomato paste
2 T. Worchestershire Sauce (p. 12)
1 T. dried parsley
2 T. dried onion flakes
2 tsp. dried granulated garlic
1/2 tsp. salt
1/2 tsp. pepper

Mix all ingrdients together in a large bowl and form inta six or eight patties.

Cook on a well-oiled skillet or grill over medium-high heat until one side starts ta brown and firm up (three to five minutes), then flip over, and cook the other side.

Serve hot on fresh buns (p. 42) with yer favorite fixins—this might be an ideal time ta give some Bourbon Whiskey BBQ Sauce (p. 18) a shot!

BLACK BEAN AND
SWEET POTATO BURRITOS

A different style a' burrito that's quick to make, mixin' sweet and spicy flavors with Salsa (p. 15), Almost Sour Cream (p. 17), green onions, and cilantro to top it all off!

prep: 5 min | cook: 10 min | makes: 6-8 servings

Flour Tortillas (p. 22)
1 T. canola oil
1/2 C. onion, chopped
1 clove garlic, minced
3 T. peanut butter
3 C. sweet potatoes, cooked and chopped
1 1/2 C. black beans, cooked and drained
1 tsp. cumin
1/2 tsp. cinnamon
1/4 tsp. cayenne pepper
1/4 C. green onions, chopped
2 T. cilantro, chopped
Salsa (p. 15)
Almost Sour Cream (p. 17)

Heat oil in a skillet over medium-high heat. Sauté the garlic and onion a few minutes until tender and onion is translucent.

Stir in peanut butter, sweet potatoes, and black beans, mashing slightly.

Add in the spices and mix well, cooking a few more minutes until all the ingredients are heated through. Stir occasionally to prevent scorching.

Serve in warm tortillas and top with salsa, sour cream, green onions, and cilantro.

BREAKFAST BURRITOS

Here's a hearty Southwestern breakfast for ya, with a bit of spice ta start yer day off.

prep: 16 min | cook: 35 min | makes: 6-8 servings

Flour Tortillas (p. 22)
2 T. canola oil
1/2 C. onion, chopped
1 clove garlic, minced
1 red bell pepper, sliced
1 C. mushrooms, sliced
1 C. corn kernels
1 carrot, peeled, chopped, and steamed tender
1 potato, peeled, cubed, and steamed tender
1 1/2 C. black beans, cooked/drained
1 1/2 C. diced tomatoes with juice
1/2 tsp. chili powder
1 tsp. cumin
2 T. brown sugar
1/2 tsp. turmeric
1/8 tsp. salt
2 T. all-purpose flour

Heat oil in a large skillet over medium-high heat; sauté onion and garlic until tender.

Add bell pepper and mushrooms and sauté a few minutes before adding all remaining ingredients <u>except</u> fer the black beans and flour.

Stir well and heat through, then reduce heat and simmer for ten to fifteen minutes.

Add black beans and sprinkle in flour, stirring well. Simmer another ten minutes or until mixture thickens. Serve in warm tortillas and get yer day kicked off right!

TACO AND BURRITO FILL
Great in Flour Tortillas (p. 22), and also used Nachos (p. 76), and Enchiladas (p. 77).
prep: 10 min | cook: 45 min | makes: 4-6 servings

1 C. TVP granules, dry
2 C. boiling broth
      (vegetable or beef-style)
1 T. canola oil
1 onion, chopped
2 cloves garlic, minced
1 red bell pepper, chopped
1 1/2 C chopped tomatoes
      with juice
1 T. Worcestershire Sauce
      (p. 12, optional)
2 tsp. chili powder
1 tsp. paprika
1/2 tsp. cumin
1/2 tsp. oregano (optional)
1/2 tsp. garlic powder
1/2 tsp. salt
1/8 tsp. black pepper
1/8 tsp. cayenne pepper

Combine TVP granules with 1 C. boiling broth, spices, and Worchestershire Sauce in a small bowl and set aside.

In a skillet over medium-high heat, sauté onion and garlic in oil about five minutes, then add the bell pepper and sauté for another few minutes so it softens a bit.

Add the remaining ingredients, including rehydrated TVP granules.

Add remaining 1 C. of broth, mix well, and bring it to a boil fer them flavors to mix.

Reduce heat and simmer uncovered 20-30 minutes, stirring occasionally until the liquid reduces and it thickens. Serve in taco shells, tortillas, or with corn chips.

FAJITAS

Here's a simple Southwestern-style wrap ta fill ya up at the end of the day.
prep: 4 min | cook: 10 min | makes: 4-6 servings

Flour tortillas (p. 22)
1 package firm/extra-firm tofu, sliced in
**   finger-size strips and marinated**
**   in chicken or beef-style marinade (p. 13)**
2 T. canola oil
1/2 onion, sliced
1 red bell pepper, sliced into strips
1 garlic clove, minced
Guacamole (p. 17)
shredded lettuce
fresh tomatoes, chopped
fresh cilantro (optional)
fresh lime wedges or lime juice (optional)

Heat oil in a skillet over medium-high heat and sauté onion and garlic about five minutes, then add bell pepper and tofu strips.

Cook until tofu strips are slightly browned and bell pepper is tender, stirring and tossing often to prevent burning.

Serve on warm tortillas and topped with guacamole, lettuce, and tomato.

Top off with a dash of lime juice and some fresh cilantro if ya dare.

NACHOS

Try this as just layered dip fer chips if ya prefer not havin' em go soggy while ya eat.
prep: 10 min | makes: 6-8 servings

1 bag corn chips
Refried beans (p. 49)
Taco and Burrito Fill (p. 75)
Cheese sauce (p. 12)
Guacamole (p. 17)
Almost Sour Cream (p. 17)
Salsa (p. 15)
1/2 C. green onions, chopped
1/2 C. fresh tomatoes, seeded and diced

Place some corn chips on a large plate, makin' a slight pit in the middle of 'em.

Spoon refried beans into center. Cover refried beans with some of the cheese sauce. Spoon taco fill on top, then cover with remaining cheese sauce. Top with salsa, guacamole, and sour cream, garnishing with shallots and tomatoes.

ENCHILADAS

This is a good end-all, be-all meal fer packs a' hungry banditos—it ain't failed me yet.

prep: 15 min | cook: 45 min | makes: 4-6 servings

Corn Tortillas (p. 23)
Some or all of the following for filling:
 - Refried Beans (p. 49)
 - Spanish Rice (p. 49)
 - Taco and Burrito Fill (p. 75)
Cheese Sauce (p. 12)
Chili Gravy (p. 15)
Salsa (p. 15)
Guacamole (p. 17)
Almost Sour cream (p. 17)
shredded lettuce
fresh tomatoes, chopped
green onions, sliced

Preheat oven to 350° F (175° C) and grease an eight-inch (20 cm) square baking pan.

Spoon yer preferred fillings along with cheese and/or chili sauce into the tortillas.

Roll each filled tortilla closed and place in baking dish with the seam facin' down.

Once the baking dish is full, pour the remaining cheese and chili sauce overtop the filled tortillas you've got packed together, spreading it around evenly with the back of a spoon ta make sure all the tortillas are covered.

Cover the whole thing in aluminium foil and bake in the preheated oven for 45 minutes.

Serve topped with the salsa, guacamole, and all the rest a' them tasty fixins!

SUMMER VEGETABLE ENCHILADAS
A tasty enchilada chock full of seasonal vegetables and tofu with a tangy sauce.
prep: 15 min | cook: 45 min | makes: 4-6 servings

6 Flour Tortillas (p. 22)
4 C. water
a dash of salt
1 C. zucchini, chopped
1 C. carrot, peeled and chopped
1 C. potato, peeled and cubed
1 medium onion, finely chopped
2 T. canola oil
1 C. firm/extra firm tofu, marinated
    beef-style (p. 13) and drained
1 T. parsley
1 1/2 C. diced tomatoes with juice
1 1/4 C. broth, vegetable or beef flavor, separated

Bring 4 C. of water and a dash of salt to boil, then add the chopped zucchini, carrots, and potatoes and cook for seven to ten minutes, until tender. Drain and set aside.

Heat 2 T. oil in a skillet over medium heat and sauté onion until softened, then add the tofu and parsley, cooking until onion is translucent and tofu begins to brown.

Add diced tomatoes and 1/4 C. of broth and bring to a boil, then reduce heat and simmer until most of the liquid is reduced; stir occasionally to prevent burning and remove from heat once enough liquid is gone that it's no longer a soupy consistency.

With the filling cooked, now it's time ta get our sauce in order. You'll need:

1 C. broth (which ya shoulda separated out above)
2 T. chili powder
1 T. tomato paste
1 T. all-purpose flour
1/2 tsp. cumin
1/2 tsp. salt
1/4 tsp. cinnamon
1/8 tsp. cloves
2 T. canola oil

Whisk all ingredients together in a saucepan and bring to a boil, continuing ta boil, and stir until the mixture begins ta thicken up.

Remove from heat and allow to cool, whisking occasionally.

(continued on next page)

(Summer Vegetable Enchiladas, continued)

Preheat oven to 350° F (175° C) and grease an eight-inch (20 cm) square baking pan and spread a couple tablespoons of the enchilada sauce around on the bottom.

Take a flour tortilla and spread a spoonful of sauce down the center of it, then fill the center with 1/6 of the filling, fold the tortilla, and place in the baking pan, seam down.

Repeat fer the remaining five tortillas and drizzle the remaining sauce overtop the tortillas packed into the baking tray (use the back of a spoon to spread it around).

Cover in aluminium foil or any lid you've got handy that works and cook for fifteen to twenty minutes—until it's all heated through and the flavors have had a chance ta blend.

SLOPPY JOES

Serve this pipin' hot on toasted buns and get yerself filled right up with a hearty meal.
prep: 20 min | cook: 30-40 min | makes: 6-8 servings

1 C. TVP granules, dry
2 T. canola oil
1 medium onion, diced
1 T. minced garlic
1 C. mushrooms, sliced
1 red bell pepper, diced
1 green bell pepper, diced
1 1/2 C. diced tomatoes with juice
1/2 C. ketchup
2 T. Worcestershire Sauce (p. 12)
1 T. tomato paste
1/2 tsp. black pepper
1/4 tsp. salt
Burger Buns (p. 42), split and
    toasted

Combine TVP granules with 1 C. hot water in a bowl and set aside to soak.

Heat oil in a skillet over medium-high heat and sauté the onion, both bell peppers, and garlic for about five minutes. Add mushrooms and cook for another few minutes before adding in yer remaining ingredients.

Stir well and reduce heat, simmering for ten to twenty minutes, until it reduces and thickens a bit. Serve hot on toasted buns.

COUSCOUS AND ROASTED VEGETABLES WITH DRESSING

This may be a bit involved, but it's a helluva dish that even tastes great cold.

prep: 15 min + 5 min | cook: 15 min | makes: 4-6 servings

1/4 C. + 2 T. olive oil
2 C. frozen carrots and cauliflower
1 1/2 tsp. rosemary, finely chopped
1/2 tsp. salt
1/4 tsp. black pepper
1/4 C. orange juice
1 tsp. cumin
2 T. white wine vinegar
2 tsp. dijon mustard
1 1/2 C. vegetable broth
3/4 C. couscous, uncooked
1/4 tsp. crushed red pepper flakes
1 C. fresh tomatoes, seeded and diced
1 1/2 C. kidney beans, cooked and
      drained well
3 T. pine nuts
1/3 C. basil leaves, sliced into thin strips

Preheat oven to 400° F (200° C) and grease a baking pan.

In a large bowl, combine frozen vegetables with 1 tsp. of the rosemary and toss.

Drizzle with 2 T. olive oil, sprinkle with salt and pepper, and toss again to coat.

Spread vegetables in a single layer on the baking pan and bake for twelve to fifteen minutes, until lightly browned and tender but still crisp enough ta snap if ya bend 'em.

While vegetables are cooking, get a small bowl and combine remaining olive oil and rosemary with orange juice, cumin, mustard, and vinegar. Blend well and set aside.

In a medium saucepan, bring the broth to a boil. Remove from heat and stir in couscous and red pepper flakes. Cover and let stand fifteen minutes.

In a large bowl, combine roasted vegetables with basil strips, beans, tomatoes, and pine nuts. Toss lightly to mix. Fluff couscous with a fork and add to the bowl along with the dressing.

Mix well and serve warm, but don't be afraid ta serve cold if it comes ta that!

BISCUITS AND GRAVY

A beloved staple of southern breakfasts and any diner worth its salt—serve it up!

prep: 5 min | cook: 20 min | makes: 6 servings

fresh Country-Style Biscuits (p. 26) or Classic Drop Biscuits (p. 32)
2 C. soy sausage, crumbled/chopped
3 T. canola oil
1/4 C. flour
3 C. soy milk
1/4 tsp. salt
1/4 tsp. black pepper

Heat oil in a skillet over medium-high heat. Add soy sausage and cook until lightly browned. Reduce to medium heat, sprinkle flour into skillet and stir well, continuing to cook until flour stuck to soy sausage is browned.

Add soy milk gradually (1/2 C. at a time), stirring constantly to ensure a smooth gravy until it thickens up. Stir in the salt and pepper and mix well.

Split one or two biscuits in half and spoon gravy overtop 'em, then dig in!

COUNTRY-FRIED TOFU

Greasy but tasty! Serve this up by itself or on buns as a fried chicken-style patty.

prep: 7 min | cook: 18 min | makes: 4-6 servings

1/2 C. oil
1 pkg. firm/extra-firm tofu, sliced 1/4-3/8 in. (1 cm) thick, pressed,
and marinated chicken-style (p. 13)
Southern-Fried Spice Mix (p. 10)
1/2 C. soy milk mixed with 2 tsp. lemon juice
2 C. bread crumbs

Place spice mixture, soy milk mixture, and bread crumbs in separate bowls.

Heat oil in a large skillet over medium-high heat.

Take each slice of tofu and dip it in the soy milk mixture, then the bread crumbs and finally the spice mixture before placing it in the skillet to cook in the hot oil.

Cook each piece until browned, then flip it over and cook the other side 'til it's a nice golden brown. Place cooked tofu slices on a plate or cooling rack lined with paper towels to soak up oil. Use extra paper towels to blot oil from top if ya'd like.

Try as a sandwich on Wholemeal Bread (p. 40) with Soy Mayonnaise (p. 18).

SPAGHETTI SAUCE

This Spaghetti Sauce is a bit like one mah momma used ta make—the whole cloves and cumin give it a richer flavor than what ya might get in a jar from yer local store.

prep: 15 min | cook: 1 hr 20 min | makes: 4 servings

2 T. olive oil
1 onion, chopped
4 garlic cloves, minced
1 red bell pepper, chopped
1 C. mushrooms, chopped
2 carrots, peeled and chopped
1 stalk celery, chopped
4 1/2 C. chopped tomatoes
      with juice
1/2 C. tomato paste
2 tsp. salt
1 tsp. dried basil
1 tsp. white sugar
1/2 tsp. black pepper
1/2 tsp. dried oregano
1/4 tsp. cumin
1 bay leaf
2 whole cloves (optional)

Heat olive oil in a large saucepan over medium-high heat.

Sauté the onion and garlic a few minutes, until onion is translucent.

Add remaining fresh chopped vegetables and sauté another few minutes.

Stir in remaining ingredients and heat until it reaches a boil, then cover the pan and reduce heat to a simmer.

Simmer covered fer about an hour, stirring occasionally to prevent scorching.

Remove bay leaf and cloves before serving over fresh pasta or steamed vegetables.

SUN-DRIED TOMATO AND ARTICHOKE LINGUINE

This might be some simple cookin', but it's filling with a nice flavor. Give it a shot.

prep: 7 min | cook: 12 min | makes: 2-4 servings

2-4 servings fresh cooked linguine
2 T. olive oil
1 onion, chopped
3 garlic cloves, chopped
1 C. sun-dried tomatoes, chopped
2 tsp. dried basil
2 tsp. dried oregano
1 C. marinated artichoke hearts, drained and chopped
1 C. baby spinach leaves (optional)
salt and cracked black pepper (to taste)

Heat olive oil in a large saucepan or skillet over medium heat.

Sauté the onion and garlic about five minutes, then add sun-dried tomatoes, basil, and oregano.

Stir until mixed well and heated up, then add the artichoke hearts and baby spinach if ya like. Stir well again and allow it all to cook until heated through.

Serve over fresh cooked linguine with salt and black pepper added to suit yer taste.

CHIK'N AND DUMPLINGS

A classic hearty, satisfyin' meal ta fill yer belly after a cold day out on the range.

prep: 15 min | cook: 50 min | makes: 4-6 servings

**2 C. (350g) firm/extra firm tofu, marinated
chicken-style (p. 13) and well-drained
3 T. + 2 T. canola oil
1 onion, finely chopped
2 stalks celery, sliced
3 T. all-purpose flour
4 C. broth, vegetable or
          chicken-flavor
1 C. frozen mixed vegetables
1 tsp. thyme
1/2 tsp. salt
1/2 tsp. black pepper**

Heat 3 T. of oil in a large skillet or medium-sized stock pot over medium-high heat and cook marinated tofu until browned, about five to seven minutes.

Transfer the browned tofu to a bowl or plate and set aside fer later.

Heat remaining 2 T. oil in same skillet or pot over medium-high heat and sauté onion and celery until onion is translucent. Add flour and stir well to coat the onions and celery, absorbing as much oil and moisture as possible for the flour to stick to 'em.

Add the broth, frozen mixed vegetables, thyme, salt, and pepper and cover, allowing it to heat to a boil while ya get ta work on the dumplings. Fer those, you'll need:

**1 1/2 C. all-purpose flour
1 1/2 tsp. baking powder
1/2 tsp. salt
1/2 tsp. thyme
1/2 tsp. sage
2 T. margarine
1/3 C. soy milk
1/4 C. silken tofu, squeezed, drained, and mashed well or pureed**

In a medium bowl, mix together the flour, baking powder, and spices. Using two knives or a pastry blender, cut in the margarine until it resembles small crumbs.

In a small bowl, add the soy milk and tofu together and mix well. Add this liquid mixture to yer dry ingredients and mix well until it forms a bit of a wet dough.

(continued on next page)

(Chick'n and Dumplings, continued)

Once yer broth and vegetables reach a boil, reduce heat and allow to simmer fer fifteen minutes; stir and scrape occasionally to ensure there's no scorchin' on the bottom.

Now add the cooked tofu and wait a few minutes for it ta heat through and bring the whole thing back to a simmer, then we're ready ta add our dumplings.

Use a spoon to scoop out golf-ball sized chunks of the dumpling dough, and drop 'em right on top of the simmering ingredients in yer skillet or stock pot.

You oughta get five or six dumplings outta that dough—space 'em out as much as possible and simmer with the lid on or ajar for another fifteen minutes, gently stirring once in awhile ta mix the flavors and make sure there's no sticking or scorching.

To serve, spoon vegetable and tofu mix inta bowls along with one a' the dumplings.

MEATYLOAF

I reckon comfort food doesn't get a whole lot more basic and tasty than this.

prep: 20 min | cook: 45 min | makes: 4-6 servings

2 C. (350g) firm/extra-firm tofu, marinated beef-style (p. 13), well-
    drained and crumbled
1 T. canola oil
1 small onion, diced
1/2 C. quick-cooking oats (uncooked)
1 C. torn bread pieces
3 T. tomato paste
1/2 tsp. black pepper
1/2 tsp. oregano
1/2 tsp. parsley
1 1/2 C. (1 can) diced tomatoes with juice (drain for a firmer loaf)

Preheat oven to 375° F (190° C) and lightly grease a loaf pan.

Heat oil in a small skillet over medium-high heat and sauté the onion until tender, then mix all ingredients thoroughly in a large bowl and pack into the loaf pan.

Cover the top of the loaf mixture with a sauce made of the following mixed well:
2 T. brown sugar
1/2 tsp. dry mustard
1 T. tomato paste + 2 T. water (or 3 T. ketchup)

Cover the loaf pan with aluminium foil and bake for 45 minutes and serve warm.

DAWGS

It just ain't a summer barbequeue without some dawgs and burgers (pgs. 70-72)!

prep: 25 min | cook: 45 min | makes: 8-12 servings

aluminium foil
parchment paper
vegetable steamer
1 1/2 C. firm/extra firm tofu, drained
 well and crumbled fine or pureed
1 C. steamed potato, mashed
1/2 C. quick-cooking oats (uncooked)
1/2 C. all-purpose flour
2 T. tomato paste
1 T. white sugar
1 T. onion powder
1 T. Worchestershire Sauce (p. 12)
2 tsp. salt
2 tsp. white pepper (or black if unavailable)
2 tsp. paprika
2 tsp. garlic powder
1 tsp. ground mustard
1 tsp. ground coriander
1/2 tsp. dried marjoram
1/2 tsp. celery seed (ground, if possible)

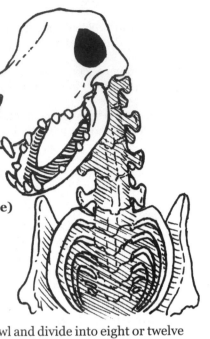

Mix all the ingredients together well in a large bowl and divide into eight or twelve chunks.

You can wrap 'em up for cooking individually or do a couple at a time depending on how wide yer parchament and foil is, but either way, this is the process, which I'll illustrate for y'all on the opposite page ta make life a bit easier for ya:

1. Tear a strip of parchment paper about six inches (15 1/4 cm) long, and a strip of foil the same length (it's okay if it's slightly longer, that'll work out better anyhow). Place the strip of parchment paper on top of the strip of aluminium foil.

2. Shape a chunk of yer dawg mix into a roll with your hands as long and wide as ya want, and place it on the parchment about 1 inch (2 1/4 cm) away from the side.

3. Shape another chunk and place it on yer parchment paper spaced the same from the other edge with a space about 1 1/2 inches (3 3/4 cm) long between the dawgs.

4. Roll the dawgs up tightly in the parchment paper.

(continued on next page)

(Dawgs, continued)

5. Roll the parchament-wrapped dawgs up away from ya in the foil, then twist the ends back towards ya ta close 'em. Finally, push the dawgs together slightly ta give ya some slack in the middle and twist the right one towards ya ta finish sealin' it up.

6. Place the foil-wrapped dawgs loosely inside a heated vegetable steamer and steam for at least 45 minutes. Allow 'em ta cool (overnight if ya can) before unwrapping and cooking 'em in a well-oiled frying pan or grill, or just heating up and eatin' as is.

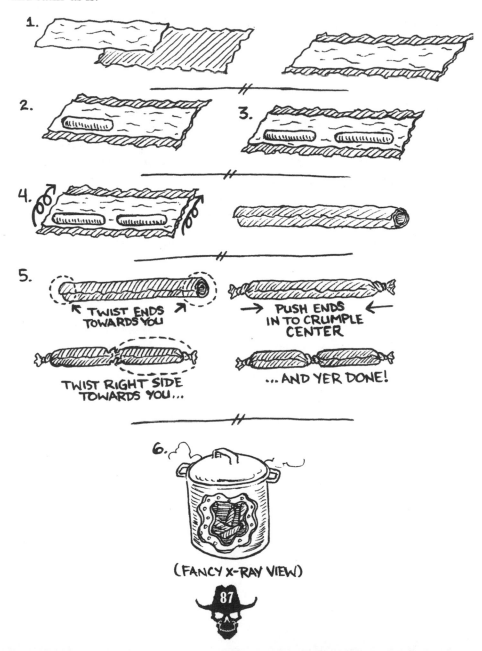

1.

2.

3.

4.

5. TWIST ENDS TOWARDS YOU

PUSH ENDS IN TO CRUMPLE CENTER

TWIST RIGHT SIDE TOWARDS YOU...

...AND YER DONE!

6.

(FANCY X-RAY VIEW)

CORNDAWGS

A star of county fairgrounds far and wide, these'll fill you up with a smile.

CLASSIC FRIED CORNDAWGS
prep: 12 min | cook: 9-18 min | makes: 6 servings

Deep fryer or deep saucepan for frying in
1 quart canola oil for deep-frying
6 Dawgs (p. 86)
1 C. all-purpose flour
1 C. cornmeal
1/4 C. white sugar
1/2 tsp. salt
1/8 tsp. black pepper
2 tsp. baking powder
1 egg substitutes—mix together well before adding:
 1 tsp. baking powder + 1/2 tsp. baking soda
 + 2 T. all-purpose flour + 3 T. water
1 C. soy milk
6 wooden skewers (popsicle sticks or even chopsticks'll do in a pinch)

If you've got a deep fryer, get yer oil in it and warmin' up to 375° F (190° C). If you'll be usin' a deep saucepan, wait until you're ready so you can keep an eye on it.

Mix flour, cornmeal, sugar, salt, pepper, and baking powder in a medium-sized bowl.

Stir in the egg substitute and soy milk—mix gently so ya don't toughen up the batter.

If yer gonna be using a deep saucepan for frying, go ahead and get that warmed up to 375° F (190° C).

Once yer oil is heated, pat each dawg dry as can be with a paper towel then jab yer dawg with a skewer and hold it straight up in the bowl of batter, spooning batter on top and twisting the dawg so the batter drips fairly evenly down the sides to cover.

Lift the battered dawg out of the bowl and get it in yer hot oil, frying three to five minutes until golden brown on all sides. I reckon two at once is about as many as you wanta try and fit in—don't crowd 'em up by trying to fry too many at a time.

Allow any extra oil ta drip off the dogs into a smal bowl (NOT over the hot oil—ya really don't want that splashin' yer way from a dropped corndawg, pardner!), then cool on a rack covered with a couple paper towels ta blot some of the oil.

Serve warm with ketchup, mustard, and any other of yer favorite other dippin' sauces.

(continued on next page)

(Corndawgs, continued)

BAKED CORNDAWGS
prep: 25 min | cook: 15-20 min | makes: 6 servings

6 Dawgs (p. 86)
1 C. all-purpose flour
1 C. cornmeal
1/4 C. white sugar
1/2 tsp. salt
1/8 tsp. black pepper
1 tsp. baking powder
6 T. margarine
1/2 C. soy milk
**6 wooden skewers (you can substitute other sticks
　　　　　　or heck, just leave 'em out)**

Preheat oven to 400° F (200° C) and lightly grease a cookie sheet or line it with parchament paper.

Mix together flour, cornmeal, sugar, salt, pepper, and baking powder in a large bowl.

Cut the margarine into the flour mixture using two knives or a pastry blender 'til the mixture resembles the usual "coarse crumbs" we're after fer these sort of doughs.

Stir in the soy milk and mix well until dry ingredients are fully moistened and you've got a dough ta work with—don't be afraid ta get yer hands in there and mix it up!

Separate the dough inta six equal-sized balls and roll each out on a lightly floured surface—or between the cut plastic bag you use for tortillas (p. 21)—until it's about 1/4 inch (2/3 cm) thick, plus long and wide enough to wrap around a dawg.

Stick a dawg firmly on a skewer and lay it in the center of a rolled section of dough, then wrap the dough around it. Press edges and holes closed and finish shaping it with yer hands. Place it on yer cookie sheet and do the same with the other dawgs.

Bake for fifteen to twenty minutes until they start browning. Serve warm with any of the usual condiments or dipping sauces ya prefer.

BREAKFAST LINKS
Made along the same lines as Dawgs (p. 86), a breakfast standard for ya ta enjoy.

prep: 25 min | cook: 45 min | makes: 12-16 servings

aluminium foil
parchment paper
vegetable steamer
1 1/2 C. firm/extra firm tofu, drained
 well and crumbled fine or pureed
1 C. mashed potato
1/2 C. steamed red bell pepper, mashed
1/2 C. quick-cooking oats (uncooked)
1/2 C. flour
1/4 C. dried minced onions
2 T. tomato paste
1 T. brown sugar
2 tsp. salt
2 tsp. dried parsley
1 tsp. black pepper
1 tsp. dried marjoram
1 tsp. dried basil
1 tsp. dried sage
1 tsp. chili powder
1 tsp. chili flakes (or to taste)
1/2 tsp. cayenne pepper (optional)
1/4 tsp. dried thyme

Mix all the ingredients together well in a large bowl and divide into twelve or sixteen chunks.

Now you'll wanta follow the same shaping and rolling steps as fer Dawgs (p. 86), but spacing out three portions along the width of the parchment paper insteada just two. I apologize fer not reprinting the same instructions here, but I thought ya might prefer more recipes than me repeatin' myself fer no real good reason.

As with the Dawgs, you'll wanta place yer wrapped breakfast links loosely inside a preheated vegetable steamer and steam 'em fer a good 45 minutes.

Allow 'em ta cool a bit (or overnight) before unwrapping 'em. Also like the Dawgs, you can eat 'em as is, or fry 'em a bit in a well-oiled frying pan or grill.

VEGETABLE POT PIE

A hearty pie of tofu, vegetables, and gravy inside a flaky crust ta fill ya up at supper.

prep: 11 min | cook: 45 min | makes: 4-6 servings

2 Pie Crusts (p. 104)
1/4 C. flour
1 tsp. salt
1/8 tsp. black pepper
1 T. nutritional yeast
3/4 tsp. garlic powder
2 C. firm/extra-firm tofu,
 squeezed dry and cubed
2 T. oil
1 onion, chopped
1 carrot, chopped
1 stalk celery, sliced
1 C. frozen mixed vegetables
2 C. Mushroom Gravy (p. 14)

Preheat oven to 375° F (190° C). Line a pie plate with one of the pie crusts and bake for ten to fifteen minutes, until starting to brown slightly. Remove from oven and set aside.

Combine flour, salt, pepper, nutritional yeast, and garlic powder. Place in a paper bag or medium-sized container with tofu and shake or toss well to coat tofu.

Heat oil in a skillet over medium-high heat and sauté tofu until lightly browned, then add the onion, celery, and carrot.

Continue to sauté until the onions are soft, then add the mixed vegetables and cook until they're slightly tender but still crisp. This should only take another five to ten minutes—try snapping a green bean now and then to see how it's goin'.

Add the mushroom gravy to the mixture in yer skillet and stir well, then transfer the whole deal to the pie plate containing the pie crust ya slightly pre-baked earlier.

Cover it all up with the second, unbaked pie crust. Seal the edges by pressing 'em together with a fork or yer fingers, and cut a few slits in the top.

Bake for 30 minutes in the preheated oven, or until top crust is lightly browned.

VEGETABLE MOUNTAIN WITH GRAVY

Sometimes a stack a' vegetables topped with tasty gravy is a perfect end to yer day.

prep: 10 min | cook: 16 min | makes: 4 servings

4 C. mashed potatoes, spiced to taste
Easy Gravy (p. 14)
2 T. oil
1 onion, sliced
2 carrots, sliced
1 C. fresh mushrooms, sliced
1/2-1 tsp. dried basil (to taste)
1/4 tsp. dried parsley
1/8 tsp. dried rosemary
salt and pepper (to taste)
1 red bell pepper, sliced
2 C. fresh spinach, chopped

Heat oil in a large skillet over medium-high heat and sauté onion a few minutes, then add carrots, mushrooms, and spices.

Sauté another five minutes, then add bell pepper, and spinach. Mix well.

Sauté until the bell pepper is a bit tender—cooked but still firm enough to snap.

To serve, spoon 1 C. mashed potatoes in a mound on a plate and mash a pit in the middle of 'em. Fill it in with the vegetables and top it all off with the gravy.

CONFECTIONERY

I'll go ahead and tell ya right now—confectionery can be one a' most maddening tasks ta undertake, at the mercy of humidity, temperature, and most of all: time. It can also be one a' the most rewarding, seeing people savor the taste of homemade candies with wide-eyed amazement when they find out there's no dairy involved.

If you're gonna roll up yer sleeves and take on the challenge, here's some tips for ya:

1. Use a candy thermometer.
After more than a few afternoons and evenings of having ta dump out a pot full of ingredients and scrapin' pans with all I've got, I learned my lesson. There ain't no two ways about it, ya oughta get yerself one or yer lookin' at a lot of needless waste and failures. Save yer sanity and enthusiasm—buy a candy thermometer!

2. Calibrate your candy thermometer.
Now that ya got a candy thermometer, ya need to make sure it's accurate or at least figure out how many degrees ya gotta adjust yer measurements, because there ain't a lot of wiggle room before yer strayin' inta the wrong candy stage.

Bring a pot of water to a rolling boil and attach your candy thermomter without the tip touching the sides or bottom. Leave it in the boiling water for ten minutes. The temperature oughta read 212° F/100° C degrees, the boiling point of water. If not, then note the difference up or down in temperature and adjust by that many degrees when following any recipes requirin' candy stage temperature ranges.

3. Use the right cookware.
Invest in a good-quality, thick-bottomed saucepot to work with. Tryin' ta use thin aluminum pots or the like for cofectionery is gonna leave ya with ruined candy at best, or a mess ta clean up and maybe some burns ta boot at worst. Make sure ya get at least a medium-sized pot or larger—some a' these recipes can really get ta bubblin' and climbin' the sides of yer pots, and ya don't want 'em spillin' over.

4. Be patient.
It ain't exactly like watchin' grass grow, but sometimes it can feel that way. Ya can't just crank up ta high heat and get there faster unless a burnt, inedible mess is what yer after. Sugar has it's own schedule, and ya just gotta tag along with it.

5. The less humidity, the better.
Even with all the right tools and patience in the world, humidity will make a difference ya just can't correct for. Try and stick ta dry days or take advantage of air-conditioning if ya got it. Results will come easier and you'll keep yer sanity.

6. Don't give up!

93

EVAPORATED SOY MILK
Prep this fer Vanilla Fudge (opposite) and Salted Bourbon Pecan Squares (p. 100).
prep: 1 min | cook: 1hr 15 min | makes: 3/4 C.

a toothpick and ink pen
2 1/4 C. soy milk

Pour 3/4 C. soy milk into a medium-sized saucepan, then dip the toothpick in until it touches the bottom of the pan and mark the height of the soy milk on the toothpick with the pen—this is yer high-milk mark for condensin' the soy milk down.

Add the remaining soy milk inta the saucepan and begin heating over medium heat, stirring once in awhile to prevent a film formin' on top.

Once the soy milk begins to boil, reduce heat to a gentle but steady simmer and keep stirrin' to avoid a thick film on top while it boils off the water content to reduce. As the soy milk visibly reduces, you'll wanna adjust yer heat down to keep the saucepan at a simmer instead a' sneakin' inta a full-blown boil.

After about 30 minutes, start checkin' the height of the simmerin' soy milk against the line marked on yer toothpick. Once the soy milk lines up with that mark, remove it from heat and stir occasionally while it cools down enough to refrigerate.

Store in refrigerator fer up to a week, but hopefully you'll put it ta use before then! Worst-case, just freeze it for later use and whisk well before using once thawed.

SWEETENED CONDENSED SOY MILK
Condensed soy milk is a must-have for Chocolate Fudge (p. 96) but can also come in handy as a substitute for sweetened cream when called for in recipes.
prep: 1 min | cook: 1hr 15 min | makes: 1 1/4 C. (14 oz)

a toothpick and ink pen
3 C. soy milk
1/2 C. white sugar

For Sweetened Condensed Soy Milk, you'll be followin' a similar process as ya did just above for plain Evaporated Soy Milk, but with the addition of sugar.

Pour 1 1/4 C. of the soy milk into a medium saucepan, then dip yer toothpick in until it touches the bottom of the pan and mark the height.

Add the remaining soy milk and the sugar into the saucepan and stir well, then heat and reduce along the same lines as the Evaporated Soy Milk instructions above.

VANILLA FUDGE

Sure it's a bit complicated, but folks couldn't tell this wasn't "real," so it's a keeper.

prep: 15 min + 2-4 hr | cook: 45 min | makes: 64 1-inch squares

3/4 C. evaporated soy milk (p. 94)
1 1/2 C. white sugar
2 T. corn syrup
1/8 tsp. salt
1/2 tsp. vanilla extract
1 1/2 tsp. margarine
parchament paper
large heatproof bowl

Grease an eight-inch/20 cm square baking pan with margarine and line it with enough parchment paper ta hang over the edges for handles, about an inch on both sides.

Coat the placed parchment paper with margarine as well and set it all aside.

Mix the evaporated soy milk, sugar, corn syrup, and salt (but not vanilla extract or margarine) in a medium saucepan. Stir over medium-low heat until sugar dissolves.

Raise the heat to medium and bring the ingredients to a boil. This part will take the longest, but hang in there and be patient. If you're gettin' particularly antsy or the weather's not in yer favor, nudge the heat up slightly ta give yer heating some help.

Once it begins ta boil, attach yer candy thermometer to the pan and continue cooking the mixture until it reaches about 238° F (114° C), right in the "soft-ball" stage.

Now with yer normal dairy fudges, ya always get instructed not ta stir as the mixture heats up ta the target temperature. However, I stir quite often and my confectionery never seems particularly worse for the wear, so make of that what you will.

Once yer temperature has reached where it needs ta be, pour the mixture inta the large heatprof bowl, then add the vanilla extract and margarine to it and gently mix it all, continuing to mix until the fudge starts to cool and thicken, ten to fifteen minutes. Ya should notice it lose some of the glossy surface it had when ya first poured it in.

Once ya feel it's noticeably cooled and thickened, pour, and scrape the contents of the bowl inta yer prepared square baking pan lined with greased parchment paper.

Chill fer two to four hours and then keep refrigerated until ready ta serve. When the time comes, lift the fudge out of the pan by the extra parchment paper on the sides and cut inta squares about an inch (2.5 cm) in size.

Keep cool when not eatin' or servin' it!

CHOCOLATE FUDGE

A different style a' fudge than yer vanilla variety, but nowhere near as complicated.

prep: 3 min + 2-4 hr | cook: 20 min | makes: 64 squares

1 1/4 C. sweetened condensed soy milk (p. 94)
3 C. dark chocolate chips/chunks
1 1/2 tsp. vanilla extract
a dash of salt
1 C. chopped nuts (optional)

Line an eight-inch/20 cm square baking pan with either aluminium foil or lightly-greased parchament paper.

Heat condensed soy milk with salt and chocolate chips/chunks in a medium saucepan over low heat, stirring until the chocolate is melted and you've got a smooth mixture.

Remove chocolate mixture from heat and stir in the vanilla.

Mix in nuts if you'll be using them, then scrape it all into yer lined square pan.

Chill the pan for two to four hours until firm, then lift out and cut into one-inch squares.

CONFECTIONERY
BUCKEYES

If ya like peanut butter and chocolate, you're gonna find a piece of heaven in these!

prep: 45 min | cook: 15 min | makes: 24 candies

24 toothpicks
1/3 C. margarine, softened
1/2 C. peanut butter
2 C. powdered sugar
1/8 tsp. vanilla extract
1 1/3 C. chocolate chips
            or chunks

In a large bowl, add margarine, peanut butter, sugar, and vanilla together. Mix well until ingredients become a thick, dough-like mass.

Line a cookie sheet with parchament paper (or just lightly grease the sheet) and roll the dough into 24 balls a bit less than 1 inch (2 1/2 cm) around.

Place each ball on the cookie sheet and spear each one deeply with a toothpick.

Once the dough is all rolled, place the full cookie sheet of speared peanut butter balls in the freezer ta chill fer 30 minutes and firm up around their toothpick handles.

After 30 minutes, melt chocolate in a bowl overtop a saucepan of lowly-simmering water or in a double-boiler if ya happen ta have one.

Stir until smooth and keep it warm over heat to prevent it from firmin' up on ya while yer usin' it in the next step.

Remove the chilled peanut butter balls from the freezer and use the toothpick in each to lower them inta the melted chocolate and mostly cover—leave a small circular area around the toothpick handle bare ta make the "eye" part of "buckeye."

Lift 'em out of the chocolate and allow a bit of the excess chocolate ta drip off before placing it back on the cookie sheet to cool. You'll wanta work fast ta keep the peanut butter mix from thawin' too much and losin' its grip on the toothpick handle.

Once they're all dipped and back onta the cookie sheet, all that's left is ta wait fer the chocolate ta cool, then remove the toothpick handle and smooth over the hole where it was stuck inta the peanut butter mix.

Refrigerate 'em until ready ta serve!

PEANUT BRITTLE

If you or yer gang like peanuts and crunchy sweets like this classic, then yer in luck!

prep: 3 min | cook: 45 min | makes: 1 cookie sheet

candy thermometer
1/2 C. white sugar
1/4 C. corn syrup
2 T. water
1/4 C. margarine
1/2 C. peanuts, raw/unsalted
 and shelled without skins
1/4 tsp. baking soda

Lightly grease a cookie sheet and place it near the stove where you'll be cooking.

Measure out the peanuts and baking soda into separate containers for quick addition.

Combine the white sugar, corn syrup, and water in a medium saucepan over medium-high heat and cook until the sugar has dissolved, leavin' ya with a syrup of sorts.

When the liquid in the saucepan starts to boil, add in the margarine, and stir well.

Increase the heat and begin monitorin' the temperature with yer candy thermometer.

Start stirring frequently once the temperature reaches 230° F (110° C).

When the mixture reaches 280° F (137° C), stir in the peanuts and stir constantly until the temperature reaches 305° F (151° C)—the "hard crack stage."

Remove the mixture from heat and stir in the baking soda, mix well to distribute it through the peanut mixture and you oughta notice a change in color and consistency.

Pour the hot mixture onta yer prepared cookie sheet and spread around as best you can while it's still hot. You can try usin' a couple cooking utensils to stretch it out from the edges, or just start mashin' it down from the center and work yer way out.

Loosen the peanut brittle from the cookie sheet and break apart into small pieces as soon as it's cool enough to handle without burnin' yerself.

Transfer ta parchment paper or another heatproof plate to finish coolin'.

Store in an airtight container and enjoy the crunchin' away when ya feel like a treat!

ALMOND TOFFEE

Tasty classic toffee with chocolate and almonds ta richly satisfy yer sweet tooth.

prep: 20 min | cook: 45 min | makes: 1 cookie sheet

candy thermometer
1 1/2 blanched, peeled almonds (see note), roughly chopped and
divided
1 C. margarine
1 1/2 C. white sugar
3 T. corn syrup
3 T. water
1 tsp. vanilla extract
1 C. chocolate chips/chunks (optional)

NOTE: If blanched, peeled almonds ain't easy ta come by in your neck of the
woods, it's easy ta do yerself with whole, skinned almonds: place 'em in a medium-
sized, heatproof bowl and cover with boiling water for one minute. Then drain
and cool under cold water and pat dry. After all that, you oughta be able ta just
squeeze one of 'em and have it shoot right outta its skin—best ta keep yer other
hand ready ta catch it! Give the peeled almonds an extra pat dry before usin'.

Preheat oven to 375° F (190° C) and spread the chopped almonds on a cookie
sheet, then bake 'em until golden brown (should take five to ten minutes). Set 'em
aside fer now.

Grease a cookie sheet (even the one ya just used) and set it aside at the ready.

In a medium-sized saucepan, combine the margarine, sugar, corn syrup, and
water.

Cook over medium heat, stirring constantly. Once it's bubbling, start makin'
use of yer candy thermometer and slowly increase the heat in small amounts as
needed until the mix measures 300° F (149° C), in the "hard-crack" stage.

Remove the mix from heat and stir in the vanilla extract along with 1 C. of the
almonds ya toasted earlier. Pour the mix out on the greased cookie sheet ya
oughta have ready ta go; flatten the toffee down and spread it out with a heatproof spatula or any other utensil you've got handy that'll do the trick.

Melt chocolate in a bowl sittin' on top of a saucepan of lowly-simmering water
(or with a double-boiler) until it's mostly melted with small blobs of chocolate
still in it.

Spread the melted chocolate over the toffee and scatter the rest of yer almonds on
top, pressing 'em down so they'll be firmly stuck in there when the chocolate fully
cools. Allow ta cool through and let the chocolate is firmly set before removing the
toffee from the cookie sheet and breaking it inta pieces.

Store in an airtight container and keep cool or refrigerated before serving.

SALTED BOURBON CARAMEL PECAN SQUARES

Dangerously, belligerently delicious treats fer the older folks yer ridin' the trail with.

prep: 5 min | cook: 45 min | makes: 64 1-inch squares

candy thermometer
1 C. evaporated soy milk (p. 94)
2 T. margarine
1/2 tsp. salt
1 1/2 C. white sugar
1/4 C. water
1/4 C. corn or maple syrup
1 T. bourbon
2 C. pecans, roughly chopped
2 T. coarse salt

Lightly grease an eight-inch (23 cm) square pan and layer the bottom with the pecans.

In a small saucepan over medium heat, mix the evaporated soy milk, margarine, and salt together and begin heating to a simmer while you move onta the next bit here.

In a medium saucepan mix the sugar, water, and syrup together and begin heating over medium heat with the candy thermometer attached—you're aimin' to heat this mixture to the caramel stage at 320° F (160° C) before moving on.

Once the caramel stage is reached, remove the saucepan from heat and drizzle in the soy milk mixture slowly while whisking quickly ta keep it from bubbling over.

WARNING: I ain't fooling around about that last step and you shouldn't be either—the scalding hot sugar is gonna want ta froth right up when you're adding the soy milk mixture in, so take care ta drizzle it in slowly while whisking quickly!

With the soy milk added in, return yer goodie-filled saucepan to the heat and use yer candy thermometer ta continue cooking until it's reached the hard-ball stage in the range of 245-255° F (118-124° C).

Stir in the bourbon and remove from heat, then pour the whole thing evenly over the pecan base in yer square baking pan.

Sprinkle the coarse salt overtop the whole thing and allow to cool fer at least a few hours before cutting.

CANDIED WINTER NUTS

Sweet mixed nuts with a hint of spice ta get ya through the cold winter months.

prep: 8 min | cook: 20 min | makes: 2 C.

2 C. mixed nuts (almonds, pecans, peanuts, cashews, hazelnuts)
1 T. margarine, melted
1 T. maple syrup or corn syrup
1/4 C. brown sugar
1 tsp paprika
1/2 tsp. cocao powder
1/2 tsp. cinnamon
1/8 tsp. cayenne pepper
1 tsp. coarse salt

Preheat oven to 350° F (175° C)

Spread nuts on a cookie sheet and bake in oven for ten minutes to lightly toast.

Mix melted margarine, maple or corn syrup, brown sugar, paprika, cocoa, cinnamon, and cayenne pepper together in a small bowl.

When the nuts have finished toasting, transfer them to a large, heatproof bowl and pour the spiced syrup sauce over them, tossing the nuts to coat evenly. Add the salt and toss again before spreading the coated nuts back on to the cookie sheet.

Bake for ten minutes or until coated nuts are browned and syrup has hardened.

Remove from oven and allow to cool thoroughly, then break up any large chunks inta manageable clusters. Store in an air-tight container ta keep fresh 'til eaten.

DESSERTS

QUICK CAKE FROSTING

A simple frosting ya kin flavor however ya like for cakes (pgs. 108-109).

prep: 6 min | makes: ~ 1 C.

2 C. powdered sugar
1/2 C. margarine
1/4 tsp. salt
2 T. water
1/2 tsp. liquid for flavor (vanilla extract, lemon juice, coffee, rum, etc.)

In a large bowl combine all of the ingredients and mix well.

Add small amounts of more sugar or water to adjust how thick yer frosting is.

CHOCOLATE CAKE FROSTING

Tasty, fudgey frosting that'll suit just about any cake, birthday, or otherwise.

prep: 7 min | makes: ~ 2 C.

3 C. sifted powdered sugar
1/4 C. + 1 T. water
1 tsp. vanilla extract
2/3 C. cocoa
1/2 C. margarine, softened

Beat 1 C. sugar, 2 T. water, vanilla, cocoa, and margarine together until creamy.

Gradually beat in remaining sugar and water until smooth, then get ta frostin'!

DESERVE'S GOT NOTHIN' TO DO WITH IT.

DESSERTS
CREAM CHEESE-STYLE FROSTING

A nut-based frosting ta slap onta yer Carrot Cake (p.59) or whatever ya like.

prep: 12 hr 15 min | makes: ~ 2 C.

food processor or blender
1 1/2 C. unsalted cashews, soaked in water for 12 hours or more
3 T. lemon juice
1 T. apple cider vinegar
4 tsp. water
1 C. powdered sugar (or to taste)
1/4 C. margarine, softened
1/2 tsp. vanilla extract
a dash of salt

I tend ta steer clear of nut-based cheesc replacements myself, but the recipe I made do with ten years ago just wasn't up ta scratch in the long run, so here's a new one. Now it ain't gonna fool anyone in a taste test, but it's a creamy frosting with a hint of lemon and vanilla that oughta fit the bill fer a carrot cake.

After soakin' the cashews in water overnight or the whole day (change the water halfway through if ya can), they oughta be plenty soft fer ya ta blend smooth.

Combine the soaked cashews, lemon juice, cider vinegar, and water in yer blender or food processor and blend the mixture until smooth.

If ya want a thicker cream-cheese substitute before makin' frosting with it, place the mixture in a square of cheesecloth (two-ply if the mesh is too wide), and hang it in a clean, room temperature location where pests won't get to it for 24 hours. Place a small bowl underneath ta catch the liquid that drips off during that time.

Place the nut cheese mixture in a medium-sized bowl and add in the powdered sugar, margarine, vanilla, and a dash of salt.

Mix well and refrigerate to allow it ta firm up a bit before using it on cakes.

DESSERTS

CARAMEL TOPPING

It takes a bit of time, but you'll have a caramel sauce to use for ice cream, cakes, or as an essential ingredient in recipes like Caramel and Cranberry Date Bars (p. 107).

prep: 1 hr | makes: 1 C.

2 C. soy milk
1 C. icing sugar
3 T. margarine
a toothpick and ink pen

Pour 1 C. soy milk into a small saucepan. Dip the toothpick straight down in the saucepan until it touches bottom. Use the ink pen to mark height of the soy milk on yer toothpick—now you've got a measuring stick for reducing. Add remaining soy milk to the saucepan and bring to a boil. Reduce heat and simmer until it reduces to the level marked on yer toothpick, about 20-25 minutes. Stir regularly and watch to prevent boilover—briefly lift off heat and stir if that's gonna happen.

Add the icing sugar and margarine, stirring well until sugar is dissolved and margarine melted. Reduce heat to barely simmering, and continue heating and stirring another fifteen to twenty min. until color is darker brown and it starts to thicken—it will thicken more as it cools. Remove from heat and use warm or refrigerate for later (just warm it up slightly and stir well before usin').

PIE CRUST

A flaky crust that's handy for dessert pies (pgs.123-125) but also good fer dinner pies (p. 91) too. Add herbs or spices in with the flour fer a bit of extra flavor.

prep: 10-30 min | makes: 1 pie crust

3/4 C. sifted flour
1/4 C. margarine
1/8 tsp. salt
1/4 T. ice water

If you place the measured ingredients in a freezer fer twenty minutes beforehand, it'll make the crust a bit easier ta work with when it's mixed.

Mix flour and salt together, then cut in margarine with two knives, or a pastry blender.

Add 2 T. of water and mix well; knead with yer hands ta ensure no pockets of dry flour are hidin' in there — only add the additional tablespoons of water if needed.

Form the dough into a ball and roll it out on a lightly floured surface to form your pie crust, then put it ta good use!

104

DESSERTS
APPLE CRISP

Just shy of a cobbler, apple crisp is an easy country dessert ta throw together.

prep: 22 min | cook: 45 min | makes: 6-8 servings

5 Granny Smith apples
1/4 C. white sugar
1 C. + 1 T. all-purpose flour
1/2 tsp. cinnamon
1 C. quick-cooking oats
1/4 tsp. baking powder
1/4 tsp. baking soda
1/2 C. brown sugar
1/2 C. margarine, melted

Preheat oven to 350° F (175° C) and have an 8-inch/20 cm square pan ready ta go.

Peel and core the apples and slice thin. Mix white sugar, cinnamon, and 1 T. flour together and mix with the apples in a large bowl and toss well to coat.

Mix remaining ingredients together well, then sprinkle half in the bottom of yer square pan, spread apple mixture over top and then cover with the rest of the mix.

Bake for 45 minutes or until topping is browned and apples baked to yer likin'.

SPICED ICE CREAM

*Try on Pancakes (p. 27), Apple Enchiladas (p. 122),
Pies (pgs. 123-125), or just on its own.*

prep: 7 min | makes: 2 C.

3 C. soy milk
3/4 C. white sugar
1 T. vanilla extract
1/2 tsp. allspice
1 1/2 C. coconut milk
1/3 C. apple juice
1 T. cinnamon
1/4 tsp. nutmeg

Whisk all ingredients together in a large bowl and pour inta a shallow pan that'll fit in yer freezer. Place the pan in the freezer and stir at hourly intervals ta ensure a smooth texture until it's totally frozen. Thaw slightly, stir and transfer to an airtight storage container keep frozen until yer ready ta use it.

COFFEE CAKE BARS

These'll spice up a cold morning on the plains and get ya ready for some wranglin'

prep: 25 min | cook: 35-45 min | makes: 24 bars

1 1/4 C. white sugar
3/4 C. brown sugar
2 C. all-purpose flour
1/2 C. margarine, softened
1/2 C. shredded coconut
1/2 C. chopped walnuts
1 tsp. baking soda
1/2 tsp. salt
1 tsp. ground cinnamon
2 egg substitutes—mix together well before adding:
   2 tsp. baking powder + 1 tsp. baking soda
   + 1/4 C. all-purpose flour + 6 T. water
1 tsp. vanilla extract
1 C. soy milk mixed with
 1 T. lemon juice
1 C powdered sugar
1-2 T. water

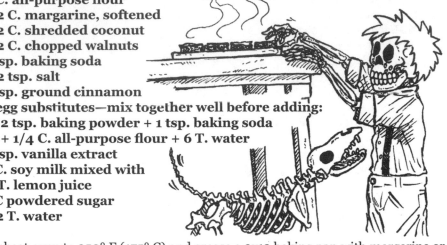

Preheat oven to 350° F (175° C) and grease a 9x13 baking pan with margarine or non-stick cooking spray.

In a medium bowl, blend sugars, flour, and margarine with a pastry blender or two knives until mixture is coarse crumbs.

Move 2 C. of the mixture to another bowl and set the rest aside.

Stir the coconut and walnuts into the 2 C. of crumb mixture and press firmly into the bottom of the greased baking pan.

Stir the baking soda, salt, and cinnamon into the bowl of remaining crumb mixture.

Add the egg substitutes, vanilla, and soy milk, mixing until well blended. Pour over the crumb base ya already pressed into the baking pan.

Bake 35-45 minutes in the preheated oven, until set and a bit spongy.

Allow to cool, then mix the icing sugar and water together to make a glaze. Add water gradually to reach a consistency yer happy with, then drizzle it onto the cake.

Allow yer glaze to set before cuttin' the cake inta bars.

CRANBERRY AND CARAMEL DATE BARS

This odd combination of cranberries, caramel and dates will knock yer socks off.

prep: 25 min | cook: 35 min | makes: 36 bars

1 C. dried cranberries, rehydrated
1/2 C. + 2 T. white sugar
2 1/3 C. all-purpose flour
2 C. rolled oats
1/2 C. brown sugar (light)
1 C. margarine, melted
1 1/2 C. dates, chopped
1 C. caramel topping (p. 104)
1/2 tsp. baking soda
3/4 C. walnuts, chopped and toasted

- If yer using whole dates, they chop easier with kitchen scissors or a knife that's been oiled or sprayed with non-stick cooking spray.

- Rehydrate dried cranberries by soaking them in water for about an hour.

Preheat oven to 350° F (175° C).

In a small bowl, combine the cranberries and 2 T. white sugar.

In a separate, large bowl combine 2 C. flour, oats, remaining sugars, and baking soda.

Add margarine and mix well. Set aside 1 C. of the mixture and press the rest firmly into the bottom of a 9x13 baking pan. Bake in preheated oven for fifteen minutes.

Get yer crust out've the oven and sprinkle on the dates, walnuts, and cranberries.

Mix caramel topping with remaining 1/3 C. flour and spoon it over the fruit and nuts.

Cover alla that upup with the remaining 1 C. of crust mixture and bake another twenty minutes or until lightly brown. Give it some time ta cool before cuttin' and eatin'!

DESSERTS
VANILLA CAKE

This'll work as a cake fer birthdays or any other occasion—frost this puppy up!

prep: 20 min | cook: 35-45 min | makes: 16-24 squares

2 C. all-purpose flour
1 T. baking powder
1 tsp. salt
1 1/2 C. white sugar
1/2 C. margarine
1/2 C. silken tofu, squeezed and pureed or mashed well
2 egg substitutes—mix together well before adding:
    2 tsp. baking powder + 1 tsp. baking soda
    t+ 1/4 C. all-purpose flour + 6 T. water
1 C. soy milk
1 tsp. vanilla extract
1/8 tsp. almond extract (optional)

Preheat oven to 350° F (175° C). Grease and flour a 9x13 pan or two 9-inch/23 cm round pans. Sift flour, baking powder and salt together in a bowl and set aside.

In a large bowl, mix sugar and margarine together until creamed light and fluffy.

Add tofu and egg substitutes then mix well. Alternate adding the flour mixture and soy milk, stirring well after each addition but not overmixin' (or it'll toughen up).

Stir in the vanilla extract and almond extract, then pour batter into prepared pan(s). Bake 35-45 minutes, until a toothpick or knife inserted into center comes out clean.

Allow ta cool before removing it from pan(s) or adding any frosting (p. 102).

CHOCOLATE CAKE

A general-purpose (chocolate variety) cake that ya kin top off with frostings (p. 102).
prep: 13 min | cook: 35-45 min | makes: 16-24 pieces

1 1/2 C. flour
1 C. white sugar
1 tsp. baking soda
1 C. cold water
1/4 C. + 1 T. canola oil
1 tsp. salt
1/4 C. cocoa
1 tsp. vanilla extract
1 T. white vinegar
1/2 C. semi-sweet chocolate bits (optional)
1/4 C. walnuts, chopped (optional)

Preheat oven to 350° F (175° C) and grease a 8-inch/20 cm square baking pan with margarine or non-stick cooking spray and lightly dust with flour.

Combine dry ingredients in a large bowl and mix well. Stir vanilla, vinegar, and oil in. When mix is completely moistened, pour in water and stir until smooth.

Fold in the chocolate bits and nuts if ya want 'em, and pour the batter into the pan.

Bake in yer preheated oven 30-35 minutes until a toothpick or knife inserted into the center comes out clean.

Allow it ta cool fully before slappin' on any frosting (p. 102).

DESSERTS
CARROT CAKE

A hefty carrot cake topped with Cream Cheese Style Frosting (p. 103)
ta take care a' yer dessert needs

prep: 35 min | cook: 35-40 min | makes: 12-16 servings

2 C. all-purpose flour
1 tsp. baking soda
1 T. baking powder
1/4 tsp. salt
1 tsp. ground cinnamon
1/4 C. silken tofu, squeezed and
 pureed or mashed well
2 egg substitutes—mix together
    well before adding:
        2 tsp. baking powder
        + 1 tsp. baking soda
        + 1/4 C. all-purpose flour
        + 6 T. water
1/2 C. soy milk mixed with
 2 tsp. lemon juice
2 T. canola oil
1 C. white sugar
2 tsp. vanilla extract
1 1/2 C. carrots, peeled and shredded
12 C. flaked/dried coconut (optional)
1/2 C. chopped walnuts (optional)
1/2 C. raisins (optional)
1/2 C. crushed pineapple, drained (optional)
Cream Cheese Style Frosting (p. 103)

Preheat oven to 350° F (175° C) and grease an 8-inch/20 cm square baking pan.

Sift the flour, baking soda, baking powder, salt, and ground cinnamon together in a small bowl and set aside.

In a large bowl, combine tofu, egg substitutes, soy milk mix, oil, sugar, and vanilla. Mix well, then add bowl of spiced flour and mix until well blended.

In another bowl, combine carrots, coconut, walnuts, raisins, and pineapple.

Stir well to evenly distribute, then fold it inta the large bowl of batter.

Pour into greased pan and bake in preheated oven 35-40 minutes, until a toothpick inserted in the center comes out clean.

Let cool before applyin' Cream Cheese Style Frosting, then chill before serving.

BREAD PUDDING

A perfect use fer bread ya got lying around, like Burger and Dawg Buns (p. 42).

prep: 20 min | cook: 45 min | makes: 6-8 servings

6 C. torn bread pieces, slightly stale (at least a day old)
2 T. margarine, melted
1/2 C. raisins
1 C. silken tofu, squeezed and pureed or mashed well and mixed with
 1/4 C. all-purpose flour
1 1/2 C. soy milk
1/2 C. white sugar
1/4 C. brown sugar
1 tsp. cinnamon
1 tsp. vanilla extract
1/4 tsp. nutmeg

Preheat oven to 350° F (175° C) and get out an 8-inch/20 cm square baking pan.

Place the torn bread pieces loosely in the pan and drizzle the melted margarine over top of them. Sprinkle the raisins evenly among the bread pieces in the pan.

In a large bowl, blend all of the remaining ingredients together and pour on top of the bread pieces, pushing the bread down with a cooking utensil ta make sure they're all good and soaked with the liquid before going inta the oven.

Bake uncovered in yer preheated oven fer 45 minutes.

Allow ta cool some before serving warm with yer favorite topping—might even wanna give some Spiced Ice Cream (p. 105) a whirl if you've got a notion.

BANANA PUDDING

Always a tasty feature at country picnics, potlucks, family reunion, this version does away with the boxed pudding and dairy but leaves plenty of flavor for ya to enjoy.

prep: 10 min + 2-4 hr | cook: 20 min | makes: 6-8 servings

one batch Vanilla Wafers (p. 120, about 48 cookies)
2 bananas
3 C. soy milk
1/3 C. white sugar
4 T. corn starch
1/8 tsp. salt
1 1/2 tsp. vanilla

Line an eight-inch/20 cm square pan with a single layer of vanilla wafers and set aside.

In a large saucepan, whisk soy milk, sugar, corn starch, and salt together.

Bring soy milk mixture to a boil, then continue whisking and boiling for at least five minutes or until the mixture gets noticeably thicker. Reduce the heat slightly if yer at risk of it boilin' over on ya, no sense gettin' burnt on account of an ornery pudding.

Remove the saucepan from heat and whisk the vanilla inta the mixture, then set that all aside ta finish preparing the pan you'll be pouring it into.

Cut a banana into slices and place a single layer of banana overtop of the vanilla wafers ya already placed in the baking pan when this whole thing got started.

Pour and spread enough of the pudding mixture to cover the wafers and bananas, then place another layer of vanilla wafers and sliced banana on top of that pudding.

Spread the rest of the pudding evenly across the top, then space out the remaining banana slices ya got over the top of the pudding before covering it all up for chilling.

Refrigerate covered for a few hours until completely firm and chilled, then serve with the remaining vanilla wafers stuck upright around the edges of the baking pan.

MIGHTY CHEWY BROWNIES

For as easy as they are to whip up, these are some mighty fine and chewy brownies.

prep: 20 min | cook: 20-25 min | makes: 24 squares

3/4 C. margarine, melted
1 2/3 C. white sugar
2 T. water
2 egg substitutes—mix together well before adding:
 2 tsp. baking powder + 1 tsp. baking soda
 + 1/4 C. all-purpose flour + 6 T. water
2 tsp. vanilla extract
3/4 C. cocoa
1 1/3 C. flour
1/2 tsp. baking powder
1/4 tsp. salt
3/4 C. walnuts, chopped (optional)

Preheat oven to 350° F (175° C).

Stir margarine, sugar, and water together in a medium-sized bowl, then add the egg substitutes, and vanilla extract.

In a separate bowl, combine the remaining dry ingredients except nuts and mix well.

Stir the cocoa mixture into the sugar mixture a bit at a time ta avoid dry clumps in yer batter, then fold in the nuts if you're optin' to use them.

Spread batter in an ungreased 9x13 baking pan and bake for 20-25 minutes.

Check 'em at twenty minutes—they're done when a toothpick stuck into the center comes out slightly sticky but fairly clean.

Whatever else ya might do, don't overcook these suckers—you'll wind up with a cocoa brick that'll just about break yer teeth off!

BOURBON BALLS

A delicious Southern staple adult treat for winter time or any ol' time!

prep: 45 min | makes: 16 balls

2 C. crumbs of crushed Vanilla Wafer Cookies (p. 120; 1 full recipe)
1 C. powdered sugar + 1/2 C. extra for rolling
2 T. cocoa
1/2 C. walnuts or pecans, chopped
1/4 C. bourbon
2 T. corn syrup

In a large bowl, stir together crumbs, 1 C. sugar, and cocoa until well combined.

Stir in nuts and mix them evenly throughout the dry crumb mixture.

In a small bowl or cup, mix the corn syrup into yer bourbon until well blended.

Add liquid into dry ingredients and mix well, then let sit with bowl covered by a dishtowel or plate for ten to fifteen minutes and allow crumb mixture ta fully absorb liquid.

When yer ready, spread 1/4 of the extra sugar on a plate or in shallow bowl. Dust the bottom of an airtight storage container with a tablespoon or two as well.

Scoop out small spoonfuls of dough and roll inta balls about one inch (2 1/2 cm) around. Roll around in the extra powdered sugar until they're coated, then place in the airtight storage container that's been dusted with sugar (ta prevent sticking).

Store in the refrigerator when done, and keep yer remaining extra sugar on hand for rolling the balls in again before servin'—the liquid's gonna soak some through the first round of sugar, but believe me they'll taste delicious for the extra trouble.

STAMPEDE COOKIES

With so much chucked inta these cookies, ah can't quite decide what kind they are, but the result is a good 'un—add or subtract ingredients ta suit yer taste.

prep: 20 min | cook: 30-40 min | makes: ~ 20 cookies

1 C. margarine
3/4 C. white sugar
3/4 C. brown sugar
1/2 C. silken tofu, squeezed and
 pureed or mashed well
1 tsp. vanilla extract
2 1/4 C. all-purpose flour
1/2 tsp. salt
1 tsp. baking soda
1/4 tsp. baking powder
1/2 C. rolled oats
1 C. chocolate chips/chunks
1/2 C. walnuts, chopped
1/2 C. shredded coconut

Preheat oven to 375° F (190° C).

In a large bowl, mix margarine, sugars, tofu, and vanilla until creamy.

In a separate bowl, combine the flour, salt, baking soda, and baking powder.

Stir the flour mixture into the sugar mixture until ingredients are well blended.

Stir in remaining ingredients and mix well. Drop dough by the spoonful onto an ungreased cookie sheet and bake fer fifteen to twenty minutes, until lightly browned.

Allow to cool before removing from the cookie sheet.

Don't fergit ta "test" a few. Ya wouldn't want yer gang windin' up with any bad cookies, now would ya?

SOFT MOLASSES SUGAR COOKIES

Classic soft and chewy molasses cookies with dark sugar and spices.

prep: 40 min | cook: 14-16 min | makes: 24 cookies

2 T. silken tofu, squeezed and
    drained well
1/4 C. white sugar
1/4 C. brown sugar
1/4 C. + 2 T. margarine, softened
2 T. molasses (not blackstrap)
1 C. all-purpose flour
1 tsp. baking soda
1/2 tsp. cinnamon
1/4 tsp. nutmeg
1/4 tsp. ground ginger
1/4 tsp. salt
1/2 C. extra white sugar (for rolling in)

In a large bowl, combine the tofu and sugars, using the sugars to grind the tofu into a smooth paste and mix well.

Add the margarine and molasses and beat until it's all smoothly blended.

In a medium bowl, mix the flour, baking soda, cinnamon, nutmeg, ginger, and salt together and mix well before adding it all to the large bowl of wet ingredients.

Mix the ingredients well until dry ingredients and fully moistened and a well-mixed dough is formed. Cover bowl and chill for twenty minutes to firm dough up.

Preheat oven to 375° F (190° C) and remove dough from refrigerator or freezer where it had been chilled. Spread the extra sugar in a shallow bowl or plate nearby.

Roll dough into balls about one-inch (2.5 cm) wide and roll in the sugar before placing on a baking sheet about two inches apart.

Bake in preheated oven for eight to twelve minutes, until edges start ta firm up.

Remove from the oven and leave 'em be fer a few minutes so they can finish cooking a bit more before ya transfer 'em to a wire rack ta cool properly.

Store in an airtight container fer a few days at most (if they ain't eaten outright!).

OATMEAL RAISIN COOKIES

Good ol' oatmeal raisin cookies, soft and chewy.

prep: 20 min | cook: 8-10 min | makes: 24 cookies

3 C. rolled oats (uncooked)
2 1/2 C. all-purpose flour
1 1/2 C. white sugar
1/2 C. brown sugar
1 tsp. baking soda
1 C. plumped raisins (see recipe)
1/2 C. silken tofu, squeezed and
 pureed or mashed well
1 tsp. vanilla extract
1/4 C. raisin water (see recipe)
1 C. margarine, melted

Preheat oven to 400° F (200° C).

Simmer 1 C. raisins in 2 C. water to plump raisins up. Drain, but keep the water.

In a large bowl, mix together the oats, flour, sugars, and baking soda.

Stir in yer drained raisins, then stir in the tofu, vanilla, and 1/4 C. raisin water.

Finally, add the melted margarine and mix thoroughly.

Drop by heaped tablespoons onta cookie sheets and bake fer eight to ten minutes but don't make the mistake of overbakin' until browned or you'll lose the chewy softness!

Store in an airtight container ta keep from drying out (or just eat 'em quicker!).

PEANUT BUTTER COOKIES
Peanut butter cookies just like Mom used ta make.

prep: 18 min | cook: 12-14 min | makes: 24 cookies

1/2 C. margarine
1/2 C. chunky peanut butter
1 C. brown sugar
1/4 C. silken tofu, squeezed and
 pureed or mashed well
1 tsp. vanilla extract
1 C. all-purpose flour
1 tsp. baking powder
1/4 tsp. salt
1 C. rolled oats (uncooked)

Preheat oven to 350° F (175° C).

In a large bowl, beat together the margarine, peanut butter, and brown sugar.

Add the tofu and vanilla into the large bowl and mix well.

In a small bowl, mix the flour, baking powder, and salt together thoroughly and then add to the large bowl and stir into the peanut butter mixture.

Finally, add yer oats in and mix well until combined inta the tasty, peanut-buttery dough you're gonna have to avoid eating raw before ya get the cookies made.

Scoop out a spoonful of dough and roll into a one-inch ball, then place it on a cookie sheet and press down with the tines of a fork to indent the top and then again with the fork rotated to cross the first indentations to make a hash pattern.

Bake in the preheated oven for twelve to fourteen minutes until they're as firm as you'd like.

CHOCOLATE NO-BAKE DROP COOKIES

A tasty favorite that doesn't require much effort for a delicious result.

prep: 7 min | cook: 18 min | makes: 24 cookies

2 C. white sugar
1/2 C. soy milk
1/2 C. margarine
3 T. cocoa powder (non-sweetened)
a dash of salt
3 C. quick-cooking oats (uncooked)
3/4 C. chunky peanut butter
1 T. vanilla extract
waxed or parchament paper (two greased cookie sheets oughta work too)

Combine sugar, soy milk, margarine, cocoa, and salt in a medium-sized saucepan over medium heat.

Bring ingredients to a boil, allowing to boil just under two minutes.

Remove saucepan from heat, and stir the vanilla into the chocolate mixture.

In a large bowl, combine the oats and peanut butter and mix thoroughly, then add yer heated chocolate liquid and then mix it all up nice and good.

Drop heaped spoonfuls of the dough onto waxed/parchment paper or a couple a' greased cookie sheets if that's all ya got on hand.

Allow to cool completely and firm up before yer gang gets their hands on 'em!

VANILLA WAFER COOKIES

You'll need these on hand for Banana Pudding (p. 112) and Bourbon Balls (p. 114)!

prep: 25 min | cook: 36-54 min | makes: 48 cookies

1/3 C. margarine
1/3 C. white sugar
1/2 C. powdered sugar
1 egg substitute—mix together well before adding:
 1 tsp. baking powder + 1/2 tsp. baking soda
 + 2 T. all-purpose flour + 3 T. water
1 tsp. vanilla extract
1/8 tsp. salt
2 T. water
1 C. + 5 T. all-purpose flour
3 T. corn starch
1 1/2 tsp. baking powder

Preheat oven to 325° F (165° C) and have two cookie sheets ready to go if you can.

In a large bowl, beat together margarine, sugars, egg substitute, vanilla, and salt until ingredients are a creamy consistency. Mix in water and whisk ta blend throughout.

In a small bowl, mix flour, corn starch, and baking powder together well and then add to the large bowl of wet ingredients and stir until dough forms into a large ball.

Scoop out 1 tsp. worth of dough at a time to roll into a ball, then squash slightly and place it on the cookie sheet. It'll go easier if ya got more than one cookie sheet ta empty and refill while the other is in the oven!

Bake in the oven for fifteen to eighteen minutes until cookies are lightly browned.

GOOD OL' SUGAR COOKIES

If yer itchin' ta put some cookies cutters ta use, I've got some great news for ya, pardner! Everywhere I've been in this big ol' world, this is about the simplest and most widely recognized cookie style there is. Roll 'em out and cut 'em inta shapes!

prep: 30 min + 2hr | cook: 8 min | per batch makes: 40 cookies

1 C. + 2 T. all-purpose flour
1/2 C. margarine
1/4 C. white sugar
2 T. silken tofu, squeezed and
    pureed or mashed well
1/2 tsp. vanilla extract
plastic wrap
parchament paper
cookie cutters
    (optional)

💥 Add 2 T. cocoa inta the mixture fer a chocolate variety

Cream margarine and sugar together in a large bowl. Add the vanilla and tofu, beating well to mix. Add the flour (and cocoa if yer optin' for it) and mix well until a dough forms. Split the dough in half and shape it inta two balls.

Wrap each chunk of dough in plastic wrap and refrigerate 'em fer at least a couple of hours so you'll be able ta roll it out and cut it. If you'd rather make simple circle shapes, just roll all the dough up into a tube shape to slice and chill it that way.

After a couple hours, start the oven preheating to 375° F (165° C) and cover a cookie sheet with a layer of parchament paper (even better, do this with two cookie sheets).

Take one chunk of chilled dough out of the refrigerator, but leave the other in the fridge until yer ready ta roll it out.

Knead the dough on a lightly floured surface a few times to warm it up so you can roll it out, then use a rolling pin ta roll it out to about 1/8" (1/3 cm) thick and cut inta shape with yer cutters and place on the parchament-covered cookie sheet.

Once yer cookie sheet is filled, place it in the oven and bake fer about eight minutes, until cookies are lightly browned at the edges. Remove 'em from the oven and slide the parchament sheet onto a wire rack ta fully cool.

Repeat the rollin' and cuttin' process with new parchament paper on the cookie sheets each time 'til yer done with the dough (don't fergit the chunk in the fridge!).

RUM CANDIED SWEET POTATOES

Sweet potatoes with a bit of a rum kick that only get better with age before servin'.

prep: 15 min | cook: 10 min | makes: 4 servings

candy thermometer
2 C. sweet potatoes, cooked and mashed
1/2 C. white sugar
1/4 C. water
1 tsp. cinnamon
1 tsp. vanilla extract
1/4 tsp. allspice
1/2 tsp. cocao
1/2 C. walnuts or pecans, chopped
1/2 C. chopped dried fruit
    (raisins, pineapple,
    apricots, etc.—no hard chips)
2 T. dark rum (optional)

Sure ya kin serve this immediately if ya like, but this dish tastes best when left ta age and blend flavors in the bottom of yer fridge fer at least a few days or even longer (especially if yer addin' the rum!).

Mix the sugar and water together in a large saucepan over medium heat and stir until the sugar has dissolved and turned the mix into sugar syrup.

Increase heat to medium-high and bring the mix to a boil until it reaches the "threading" stage at 225° F (110° C).

Use a candy thermometer if you've got one handy, otherwise just stir regularly and frequently lift yer spoon up—keep an eye out fer dripping sugar syrup that begins to hold its shape as strand trailing off the spoon.

Once the sugar syrup starts threading, remove it from heat, add the sweet potatoes into the saucepan and mix well—be sure to mix it in the saucepan, not a cool bowl!

Once the sugar syrup and sweet potatoes are well combined, transfer the contents of saucepan into a heatproof bowl and mix in the remaining ingredients.

Cool and then place in a refrigerator to chill in an airtight container before serving.

APPLE ENCHILADAS

A tasty excuse to use leftover tortillas—try toppin' with Spiced Ice Cream (p. 105).
prep: 30 min | cook: 30 min | makes: 6 servings

6 flour tortillas (p. 22)
1/4 C. white sugar
1/4 C. brown sugar
1 T. all-purpose flour
2 T. water
1 tsp. ground cinnamon
1/4 C. margarine
4 C. apple pie filling, canned or ya kin make as follows:
 - 4 granny smith apples, peeled, cored and sliced
 - 1/3 C. white sugar
 - 1/3 C. brown sugar
 - 1 1/2 tsp. ground cinnamon
 - 1/8 tsp. nutmeg
 - 1/4 C. all-purpose flour

Preheat oven to 350° F (175° C) and grease a eight-inch/20 cm square baking pan.

Place a few heaped spoonfuls of filling in each tortilla, then roll the tortillas up, and place 'em in the baking pan, seam-side down.

Heat water, sugars, margarine, and cinnamon, in a saucepan over medium heat. Bring to a boil, stirring constantly to prevent burning.

Reduce heat and simmer for a few minutes to let sauce thicken. Remove from heat and pour over tortillas, spreading with a spoon to ensure they are evenly coated.

Bake in the oven fer twenty minutes,
until bubblin' and golden brown on top.

Serve warm, topped with
Spiced Ice Cream (p. 105).

APPLE PIE

It's about as old-fashioned as pies get—try it topped with Spiced Ice Cream (p. 105)
to serve it a ` la mode (not "Alamo," mind you—that's another matter altogether).

prep: 20 min | cook: 60 min | makes: 6-8 servings

2 unbaked pie crusts (p. 104)
1/3 C. white sugar
1/3 C. brown sugar
1/4 C. flour
1 tsp. ground cinnamon
3/4 tsp. ground nutmeg
5 granny smith apples

Preheat oven to 375° F (190° C) and line a pie plate with one a' the pie crusts. Peel, core and slice the apples thinand set aside.

In a large bowl, combine sugars, flour, and spices. Add apples and toss well.

Pour the apple mixture into the pie plate, then cover it all with yer second pie crust, press the edges together with a fork and cut a few vents in the top.

Place on a baking sheet (to catch any spillover) in the preheated oven.

Cook for 1 hour, until filling bubbles and the apples are cooked.

PUMPKIN PIE

About the best thing ya kin ask from pumpkin, besides fresh pumpkin bread (p. 29).

prep: 20 min | cook: 60 min | makes: 6-8 servings

1 unbaked pie crust (p. 104)
2 C. pumpkin, cooked and pureed
3/4 C. white or brown sugar
1 tsp. ground cinnamon
1/4 tsp. ground cloves
1/2 C. silken tofu, squeezed and
 pureed or mashed well
1/2 tsp. salt
1/2 tsp. ground ginger

Preheat the oven to 425° F (220° C) and line a pie plate with the unbaked pie crust.

Blend all ingredients together and pour into the pie plate lined with crust.

Cook at 425° F (220° C) for fifteen minutes, then reduce heat to 350° F (175° C) and cook an additional 45 minutes until it's firm. Chill in refrigerator before servin'.

PECAN PIE

No matter how full I am from a hearty meal, I can always find room for Pecan Pie!

prep: 30 min | cook: 45-60 min | makes: 8 servings

1 unbaked pie crust (p. 48)
1 1/4 C. pecan halves
    (or chopped, if ya prefer)
1 C. white sugar
1/4 C. corn syrup
1/4 C. margarine
2 T. cornstarch mixed with
 1/4 C. water
3/4 C. silken tofu, squeezed
    and pureed or mashed well
    and mixed with:
      3 T. all-purpose flour
1 tsp. vanilla extract
1/4 tsp. salt

Preheat oven to 350° F (175° C) and just ta be safe, ya might also want ta put an empty cookie sheet in the oven to catch any spills that might occur when bakin' this.

Alright, ya got the oven on, now it's time ta git that unbaked crust settled properly in a pie plate with the pecan halves spread inta a single layer all over the bottom.

In a large bowl, combine the tofu mixture with the vanilla and salt, and set it aside.

In a medium saucepan, combine the sugar, corn syrup, and margarine together. Heat it all up over medium heat until it starts to boil.

With yer sugar mixture thoroughly boilin', add the cornstarch and water mixture in and stir well. Return it all to a boil for 2-5 minutes—stir often and reduce heat ta keep it from risin' up too high and boiling over, if necessary.

Remove the boiling sugar mix and pour it inta the large bowl of tofu mixture, stirring well and/or whisking to combine it all up thoroughly and smoothly.

Pour yer sugar mix inta the prepared pie plate, right overtop all of them pecans (trust me, they ain't gonna be lost and buried when this is all over and done with).

Place yer pie in the oven (in the center of the cookie sheet if yer usin' one) and bake for 45-60 minutes. The full 60 minutes'll get ya firm pie, or take it out earlier than that for more of an oozin' caramel-type pie. Either way, you're gonna enjoy eatin it!

DESKERTS
SWEET POTATO PIE

Not yer usual breed of pie, but once ya have a taste it'll make perfect sense to ya.

prep: 25 min | cook: 60 min | makes: 6-8 servings

1 unbaked pie crust (p. 48)
1 1/2 C. sweet potatoes, cooked and mashed
1 T. margarine, softened
1 tsp. baking powder
1/8 tsp. ground cloves
1/8 tsp. ground nutmeg
1/2 C. silken tofu, squeezed and pureed or mashed well
1 C. white sugar
1 tsp. baking soda
1 tsp. ground cinnamon
1/8 tsp. ground allspice
1/2 tsp. vanilla extract
1/2 C. soy milk with
 2 tsp. lemon juice mixed in

Preheat oven to 400° F (200° C) and line a pie plate with the unbaked crust.

In a large bowl, combine sweet potato, margarine, and dry ingredients. Beat until smooth, then stir in tofu, soy milk, and vanilla.

Pour into pie plate and bake in preheated oven at 400° F (200° C)for ten minutes, then reduce heat to 350° F (175° C) and cook an additional 35 minutes.

Serve warm or chilled and garnished with whipped topping and a whole pecan.

~ ADIOS, MUCHACHOS. ~

SUBSCRIBE TO EVERYTHING WE PUBLISH!

Do you love what Microcosm publishes?

Do you want us to publish more great stuff?

Would you like to receive each new title as it's published?

Subscribe as a BFF to our new titles and we'll mail them all to you as they are released!

$10-30/mo, pay what you can afford. Include your t-shirt size and month/date of birthday for a possible surprise! Subscription begins the month after it is purchased.

microcosmpublishing.com/bff